THE REGISTER
OF
SAINT PAUL'S PARISH
1715-1798

THE REGISTER
OF
SAINT PAUL'S PARISH
1715-1798
STAFFORD COUNTY, VIRGINIA
1715-1776
KING GEORGE COUNTY, VIRGINIA
1777-1798

* * *
* *
*

REFERENCE

ARRANGED ALPHABETICALLY BY SURNAMES
IN CHRONOLOGICAL ORDER

By
George Harrison Sanford King
Fellow, American Society of Genealogists
Fredericksburg, Virginia

1960

SOUTHERN HISTORICAL PRESS, INC.
P.O. Box 738
Easley, South Carolina 29641-0738

ISBN 0-89308-577-4

TO THE MEMORY OF

MY FRIEND

MAJOR JOHN BAILEY CALVERT NICKLIN

1891 - 1949

CONTENTS

INTRODUCTION

When I first saw the parish register of Saint Paul's Parish over thirty years ago it was in a deplorable state of repair. The back had all but disappeared, the first dozen pages were completely loose and many pages had crumbled around the edges into the writing. In 1940 the John Lee and Lillian Thomas Pratt Foundation sponsored the restoration of this volume and it is now handsomely bound in black leather with gold lettering.

The book bears the business plate of the seller:

> "DANIEL WELLES
> Stationer
> at the Crown & Scepters in great Eastcheap
> near Crooked Lane end, London
> Makes and Sells all sorts of Merchants Ac
> compt Books, Shop Books, Pocket Books &c.
> Likewise Sells all sorts of Writing & other Pa
> pers,Bills of Lading,Letter Cases & all other Sta
> tionary Wares wholesale & retale at reasonable rates"

The register begins in 1715 apparently in the handwriting of a parish clerk, and it appears there were several such clerks who were not polished penmen and who made multiple errors both in names and dates, until the Reverend David Stuart could no longer tolerate their haphazard manner. After an entry of the 6th of June 1725 he wrote:

> "Note that several of the above children's names are
> wrong inserted as to the year of God, by reason of
> the carelessness of the Clerk, which occasioned my
> taking the Register into my own Care and Management.
> David Stuart, Minister"

The Reverend David Stuart seems to have kept the register until the month of his death which took place on the 31st of January 1748/9, although as early as 1747 there are entries in the handwriting of his son the Reverend William Stuart (1723-1798).

The Reverend David Stuart was more systematic than the parish clerk whose manner of keeping the register he criticed, but neither he nor his son were beyond reproach in this duty. Both of these rectors made many errors in spelling both Christian and surnames as well as dates. Illiteracy was prevalent among their parishoners and it appears various names were recorded phonetically, not always the same way.

Both of the Reverend Mr. Stuarts were consistent, however, in spelling the surnames of the great landed families of their parish; neither errs in spelling Alexander, Ashton, Berry, Berryman, Buckner, Bunbury, Dade, Fitzhugh, Foote, Fowke, Gray, Hooe, Jones, Massey, Pratt, Scott, Seaton, Short, Stuart, Thornton and Washington. With many other surnames they were quite inconsistent and this fact has made it somewhat difficult to bring the register into the form I now present. A

ix

INTRODUCTION

verbatim transcription would not have been as useful and that too would have presented its problems.

Inconsistencies are also found in certain Christian names: Alis, Ales and Alce for Alice; Helen, Helenor, Heleanor, Eleanor and Elinor are interchanged and it appears the Reverend David Stuart often wrote Hele(a)nor for Eleanor; and we are sometimes puzzled over Hester and Esther as well as Elizabeth and Eliza. Several of the leading families in the parish were descendants of Captain Robert Beheathland, who came to Jamestown with the first settlers of 1607, and the name was often used as a Christian name in these families, yet the register sometimes errs in the spelling of the name. It appears other families in the parish, not descendants of Captain Robert Beheathland, took a fancy to the name and also used it. Other obvious errors were Grice for Price; Garry for Parry (Perry); Parrett for Barett &c. Likewise there are many inconsistencies in the dates; sometimes other more reliable contemporary records definitely show Saint Paul's Parish Register to be in error, while prima facia evidence in the register itself reveals obvious errors.

The Reverend David Stuart seems to have made entries soon after the recorded happenings in most instances, but at times there is evidence the Reverend William Stuart neglected the Register and attempted to transcribe into it, doubtless from another note book, that which should have been recorded several years previously. A careful study of the Register indicates that this practice led to confusion. Thus some doubt arises at times as to the precise year, date or name.

As examples of these alleged errors in the Register I wish to point out but a few:

1. The Register records the birth of Phillis Reilly as the 14th of November 1717, while her tombstone says she was born the 15th day of November 1717 and died the 4th day of April 1771, aged 54 years. She was the wife of Captain William Mountjoy (April 17, 1711 - September 27, 1777) of Overwharton Parish, Stafford County.

2. The Register records the death of Robert Taliaferro as the 6th of June 1726, while his tombstone at "Eagle's Nest" says:

> "Here lies the body of
> ROBERT TALIAFERRO son
> of Francis and Elizabeth
> Taliaferro who Departed
> this Life the 9th of May 1726
> in the 28th year of his age."

3. The Register records the death of Elizabeth Walker as the 25th of August 1737, while her tombstone says:

> "Here lies the Body of
> Elizabeth Walker
> wife of William Walker of Stafford
> County and daughter of Henry Netherton,

x

Gent: deceased, who departed this life
August 26, 1737 Etates 29."

The above inscription also shows the correct spelling of the surname of this lady; it will be noted that Reverend Mr. Stuart erred when he recorded their marriage in 1731. William Walker was an architect and his interesting will remains of record at Stafford County Court. The diary of the Reverend Robert Rose (1704-1751) of Essex County is enlightening concerning persons in Saint Paul's Parish as he married on the 6th of November 1740 Ann Fitzhugh (March 8, 1720/1 - April 18, 1789), daughter of Colonel Henry[2] Fitzhugh of "Bedford" and often visited in the parish. Reverend Mr. Rose recorded:

> February 28, 1748/9: Left Essex, dined at Port Royal, bound Robert Bagge to Robert Walker, got to Capt. Fitzhugh's at night.
> March 1, 1748/9: Left Capt. Fitzhugh's. Rain. Stopped at Mr. William Fitzhugh's ["Marmion"] and dined, returned to Mr. Walker's who had got home from Williamsburg where he had undertaken the Capitol for £2,600.
> February 11, 1749/50: Went to Overwharton Church where I heard of Mr. William Walker's death which will, I hope, delay the building of the Capitol. Returned to Mr. John Fitzhugh's. Very cold.
> February 15, 1749/50: Went to Mr. William Walker's funeral who was buried with his wife in one grave [at "Bedford"]. Very cold.

4. The Register records the death of Captain Samuel Bowman as July 14, 1742, while his tombstone at "Eagle's Nest" says:

"CAP[T].
SAMUEL BOWMAN
OF WHITEHAVEN
Born the 10 June
1681
Died the 18 July
1742."

5. The Register records the birth of John Burkett Pratt as 6th of August 1761 while a contemporary recording in his parent's family Bible as well as his tombstone in the family cemetery at "Camden", Caroline County, Virginia, says he was born the 4th of September 1761, and died the 15th of January 1843. He dropped his middle name and married in 1784 Alice Fitzhugh (January 20, 1759-November 28, 1845), wealthy widow of Henry Dixon, Gentleman, of Port Royal, and daughter of John Fitzhugh (1727-1809) of "Bellaire", Stafford County, and Alice Thornton (1729-1790), his wife. The lineal descendants of John and Alice Pratt are yet in possession of "Camden."

On the other hand, it appears the Register is correct in recording the marriage of Benjamin Baber to Mildred Berry on the 10th of November 1791, while the King George County Marriage Register notes the license was issued the 11th of May 1790. Likewise Reverend William Stuart recorded he married on the 23rd of November 1791 Enoch Berry and Judith Fowke, while the King George County Marriage Reg-

INTRODUCTION

ister notes the license was issued the 11th of May 1790. It is impossible for me
to say how these discrepancies came about, but it appears likely the recordings
of the Reverend William Stuart in these instances are correct.

The alteration in the Calendar which took place in 1752 will explain other
apparent discrepancies in the Register. For instance, the birth of William Fitzhugh of "Chatham" is recorded by the Reverend David Stuart as the 24th of August
1741 while a sampler made by his daughter and his tombstone inscription both record his birth as the 4th of September 1741; the former is the Old Style date and
the latter is the New Style date. It appears some people quickly adopted the New
Style or Gregorian Calendar, which was effective in England and her colonies in
1752, to reckon their birthdays and made the alteration at once while others clung
to the Old Style or Julian Calendar. Among the latter was General George Washington who was born the 11th of February 1731/2 (Old Style) or the 22nd of February
1732 (New Style); it is said he always celebrated his birthday on the 11th of February. The Virginia Gazette of the 26th of February 1780 said: "Friday, the 11th
instant, was celebrated at Fredericksburg the birthday of our illustrious Chief,
General Washington." [This newspaper account gives considerable detail of the
celebration at Fredericksburg, Virginia, where the General's mother lived.]

But now after all these years, these errors and discrepancies are trifling
matters for the most part - slips of the pen and memory. We can but be forever
grateful to those who left us Saint Paul's Parish Register, for indeed it fills
a void as no other manuscript could possibly do considering the mulitated Stafford County court records and the loss of many other records in this area.

Roughly it may be said that the Register records marriages 1715-1796; births
1715-1775 with a few thereafter; and deaths 1715-1750 with a few thereafter of
relatives of Parson Stuart and his death in 1798. The Reverend David Stuart usual-
ly recorded both birth and baptismal dates in full for whites and Negroes, but the
Reverend William Stuart records only the birth dates. After the beginning of the
Revolutionary War Parson Stuart virtually discontinued recording the births of
both whites and Negroes and for the next twenty years his entries are almost en-
tirely those of the marriages which he performed. After recording the death of
his mother, Mrs. Jane (Gibbons) Stuart who died the 14th of January 1749/50, Reverend William Stuart ceases to systematically record the deaths in Saint Paul's
Parish as had been the custom of his father for the twenty five years preceeding.

The abbreviations employed are the usual: B.(born); M.(married); D.(died).

This arrangement of Saint Paul's Parish Register is my own although it is
fashioned after an arrangement made by my late friend, Major John Bailey Calvert
Nicklin (1891-1949) of Chattanooga, Tennessee, who was for many years an ardent
student of genealogy and many of the aristocratic families of Saint Paul's Parish
commanded his attention. It is to him that I affectionately dedicate this volume.

Attention is directed to the fact that many families mentioned in the presently presented Saint Paul's Parish Register are also mentioned in the Overwharton
Parish Register (1720-1760) which was published in 1899 by the late Reverend Willia
F.Boogher, however, it must be noted that that publication is not without considerable error. That volume is long out of print and the present compiler has made a

transcription of it preparatory to issuing it in a form similiar to the presently presented Saint Paul's Parish Register.

I am indebted to the Reverend Joseph S. Ewing, rector of South Farnham Parish, Essex County, Virginia, and to Ralph Happel, Esquire, historian, The Nation-
al Park Service, for historical data which has not hitherto appeared in print.
In in the historical sketch of Saint Paul's Parish which follows, Mister Ewing
supplied the information relative to the Reverend William Stuart being minister
of South Farnham Parish 1747-1749 and Mister Happel told me of the derivation of
the name of Overwharton Parish. I have also drawn information from the published works of Bishop William Meade, George Maclaren Brydon, D.D., (Historiographer
of the Diocese of Virginia), and George Carrington Mason (Historiographer of the
Diocese of Southern Virginia).

I wish to thank the Vestry of Saint Paul's Parish for allowing me access to
the original Register and also my many friends in the Parish and elsewhere for
their encouragement in the preparation of this volume.

George H.S. King

1st of August 1960

SAINT PAUL'S PARISH .

A Historical Sketch

The Parish of Saint Paul's took its name from the English parish in Bedford-
shire, the birthplace of its leading Seventeenth Century citizen, Colonel William
Fitzhugh (1651-1701), who came to Potomac River in 1670 and settled in Stafford
County, calling his plantation "Bedford." The history of Saint Paul's Parish is
inseparable from that of the Fitzhugh family; Fitzhugh influence through many
successive generations is clearly traceable to the present day.

When Westmoreland County on the Potomac River was formed in 1653, the upper-
most parish thereof was called Potomac and extended from the junction of Machodoc
Creek with the Potomac River up the Potomac River to the falls and backward into
the forest to include all that land which was drained by the great Potomac River.
In 1664 Stafford County was formed and included all that region described above
as Potomac Parish and shortly the various records indicate that Potomac Parish
was divided into two parishes which were called "the upper Parish" and "the lower
Parish" and the dividing line between them was and is Passapatanzy Creek. Probably
by no official act but as time went on the upper parish came to be known as Stafford Parish and the lower parish as Chotank [Chotanck, Jotank &c] Parish, and
they were so designated in 1680.

Henry Peyton, Gentleman, is described in a deed of 1680 as "of Chotancke
Parish in the County of Stafford." Samuel Hayward, Gentleman, of Stafford County
by his his last will and Testament dated the 3rd of April 1684 and proved the 11th
of November 1696, bequeathed "unto ye Vestry of the Lower Parish of Stafford two
thousand pounds of Tobacco and Cask to buy something that may be ornamentall to y^e
said Church." On the 15th of August 1693 Theodorick Bland, Surveyor of Stafford
County, made a survey for Captain John Withers of "a tract of land lying in Stafford County in ye Parish of Chotank." It is thus seen that the lower parish of
Stafford County, which was to be called Saint Paul's, was known during the last
quarter of the Seventeenth Century as both "the Lower Parish" and as "Chotank Parish," taking its name from the largest creek in its limits yet called Chotank Creek
and upon whose banks stood the ancient Indian town of Chotank.

Doctor Edward Maddox by his last will and Testament dated the 23rd of June
1694 describes himself as"of Stafford Parish, Stafford County, in the Colony of
Virginia," and same was admitted to probate the 11th of December 1694. Doctor
Maddox's only child, Amy Maddox, married without his approbation, Thomas Derrick
causing the doctor to bequeath his plantation consisting of between 450 and 500
acres on Passapantanzy Creek as a Glebe for the Parish of Stafford. This act
gave rise to a chancery suit more than a hundred years later by which the descendants of Mrs. Derrick attempted to recover this valuable tract of land after the
dissolution of church properties by the Virginia General Assembly; in these papers
it is stated that the Parish of Stafford mentioned by Doctor Maddox in his will
was "later called Overwharton Parish." On the 14th of September 1698 William
Downing is described in a deed as of "the Parish of Stafford in the County of
Stafford" and all indications are that the upper parish of Stafford County [called
Stafford Parish] and the lower parish of Stafford County [called Chotank Parish]

did not officially come to be known as Overwharton Parish and Saint Paul's Parish, respectively, until shortly after 1700. The earliest recorded use of the names Saint Paul's Parish and Overwharton Parish appears to be in an official list of the Virginia parishes in 1702 and these names have survived to the present day.

Overwharton Parish derived its name from the English parish of Overwoorten in Oxfordshire where was born Colonel Henry Meese (16 -1682) who settled in Stafford County on Potomac Creek calling his plantation "Overwarton." Colonel Meese returned to England where he died and his land above mentioned came into possession of the Reverend John Waugh (1630-1706), the fiery minister of the upper parish of Stafford County. He seems to have preferred to call the plantation "Overwharton" and thus the upper parish of Stafford County derived its name. It is an odd coincidence that the two parishes of Stafford County should derive their names through two men who were for years bitter political enemies - the Reverend John Waugh, a Whig, and Colonel William Fitzhugh, a Tory.

As no list has been found of the church wardens and vestrymen of Saint Paul's Parish when it first came into existence, I wish to cite the following records which show the prominent men of the county, some of whom were certainly of the vestry of their parishes. Those whose names are marked thus [#] were residents of Overwharton Parish and those whose names are marked thus [*] were residents of Saint Paul's Parish.

By a writing dated the 30th of September 1701 at Williamsburg, Colonel Francis Nicholson, Governor of Virginia, appointed the following gentlemen as a Commission of the Peace for Stafford County:

#George Mason	*Rice Hooe	#Joseph Sumner	*William Bunbury
*Robert Alexander	*Richard Fossaker	#John Waugh, Jr.	#John West
#Mathew Thompson	*John Washington	*Edward Hart	*Charles Ellis

The following gentlemen served at various times in 1702-1703 as Justices of Stafford County:

#Colonel George Mason	#Captain Joseph Sumner	#Mr.Mathew Thompson
*Lt.Col. Rice Hooe	*Captain Philip Alexander	*Mr.Richard Foote
*Captain Charles Ellis	*Captain Thomas Clifton	*Mr.William Bunbury
*Captain Richard Fossaker	#Captain John West	#Mr. Thomas Gregg

On the 13th of March 1703 the following gentlemen signed a Memorial to Her Majesty, Queen Anne, in regard to the death of her late brother-in-law King William:

*Robert Alexander	*William Bunbury	#John West	*William Fitzhugh
*John Washington	#Thomas Harrison	#John West,Jr.	*Benjamin Colclough
#Mathew Thompson	#George Mason	#John Peake	#George Anderson
#Giles Travers	#Moses Lynton	#G. Mason	*Thomas Lund
*Richard Fossaker	#Alexander Waugh	*Thomas Gilson	*Philip Alexander
	*Charles Ellis	*Edward Hart	

In a list of the militia for the various counties of Virginia dated the 17th of June 1703, which was certified to Her Majesty, Queen Anne, the following field officers are named for Stafford County:

COLONEL: #George Mason
LT.COL.: *Rice Hooe
MAJOR : *William Fitzhugh

CAPTAINS:

*Charles Ellis
#George Anderson
#John West
#Edward Mountjoy
#Thomas Harrison
*Richard Fossaker

In 1702 the clerk of Stafford County was Major William Fitzhugh of Saint Paul's Parish; the sheriff was Captain Charles Ellis of Saint Paul's Parish and the sub-sheriff was Captain George Anderson of Overwharton Parish.

After 1702 there are frequent references in the court records to both Overwharton Parish and Saint Paul's Parish, but perhaps the earliest two such references are to be found in two deeds now of record at Stafford Court, viz: by deed dated the 22nd of March 1704 Edward Hinson is described as of Overwharton Parish and by deed dated the 11th of October 1704 Thomas Kitching is described as of Saint Paul's Parish.

While the name Saint Paul's seems to have replaced Chotank as the official name of the lower parish of Stafford County about 1702 there were those long acquainted with the region who clung to the ancient name. Doctor Gustavus Brown (1689-1762) of Charles County, Maryland, on the 31st of May 1726 made a power of attorney to "my worthy and very good friend the Reverend David Stuart, Rector of Choetank Parish in the County of Stafford in the Colony of Virginia," authorizing him to collect various debts due to him in the said colony of Virginia. In a deed dated the 7th of April 1727 from Colonel Gerard Fowke (1662-1734) of Durham Parish, Charles County, Maryland, to his son Captain Chandler Fowke (circa 1695-1745) of Overwharton Parish, Stafford County, for land on Passapatanzy Creek in Overwharton Parish, Stafford County, one of the bounds mentioned is the road which leads from "the plantation whereon John Mees now lives to Chotank Church." These references to Chotank Parish and Chotank Church indicate that although the name had been replaced by Saint Paul's twenty five years previously there were those who chose to use the former name. Even in this Century residents of Saint Paul's Parish have been referred to as Chotankers.

The bounds of the lower parish of Stafford County, called in succession Chotank Parish (ante 1680-1702) and Saint Paul's Parish (1702-1960), remained unaltered during the colonial period and included all that territory drained by the Potomac River between Machodoc Creek and Passapatanzy Creek. On the 3rd of April 1667 the Stafford County Court ordered "that the Minister preach in three particular places in this county, viz: at the Southwest side of Aquia, at the Court House, and at Choatank at the house belonging to Mr. Robert Townsend: to officiate every Sabbath day in one of these places until further order." The first two named places were in the upper parish of the newly formed county of Stafford while the house of Mr. Robert Townshend (1640-1675) stood upon his plantation, "Albion," and where his tombstone is yet to be seen. This land was patented the 7th of February 1650 by his mother, Mrs. Frances (Baldwin) Townshend, widow of Richard Townshend, Gentleman, and is described as 2,200 acres in Northumberland County lying upon the south side of Potomac River, on the east side of Chotank Creek and on the west side of Mattchotick [Machodoc] Neck and near Chotank Town. The estate fell into Westmoreland County upon its formation in 1653 and when Stafford County was severed

SAINT PAUL'S PARISH

from Westmoreland County in 1664, the land fell into that county.

From the services initiated at the house of Mr. Robert Townshend in Chotank some few years later the first church in the present parish of Saint Paul's was built on the "Bedford" estate of Colonel William Fitzhugh. The location which is traditionally pointed out for this first church is about a mile from the mouth of Chotank Creek and three miles east of the present church near the present post office of Owens.

In addition to the principal church of the parish on the "Bedford" estate there may have been a chapel or two conveniently located as Colonel Fitzhugh in a letter dated the 18th of May 1685 acknowledged a "generous gift to our Parish" made by Nicholas Hayward of London and refers to the parish's "paper-built temples" by which expression I opine the Colonel did not consider the construction of these houses of worship very sturdy. Nicholas Hayward was a brother of Samuel Hayward, Gentleman, Fitzhugh's neighbor and friend, who has been previously referred to as a benefactor of their parish church.

To a merchant correspondent in London, one John Cooper, Colonel Fitzhugh wrote in 1690, saying that his brother-in-law George Luke had not only undertaken to bring over from Christ's Hospital "an ingenious boy" educated in arithmetic to be a bookkeeper, but also had promised to find for the church at "Bedford". ."an able, learned, serious and sober minister, whose allowance here would be large and comfortable." Colonel Fitzhugh desires that if Luke should fail in these commissions, Cooper is to attend to these matters and he is apt to point out that the Bishop of London would provide the minister with a travel allowance of £20 when he sets out for Virginia.

The loss of all the parish vestry books for the colonial period makes the historian's task difficult. County records, however, fill a few gaps. We note, for instance, that John Allen, a tailor, of Saint Paul's Parish, died there on the 14th of October 1725 and by his last will and Testament dated the 11th of October 1725 bequeathed his landed estate to the parish and further provided that four Negro slaves and the remainder of his personal estate (except certain specific legacies) should be disposed of by his executors to be "laid out in purchasing land and the perquisities of the said land so purchased to be allocated and set apart for the proper use and uses of the then minister of Saint Paul's Parish aforesaid and his successors forever and that the said Minister and his successors should receive the yearly annuity of the said land and pay yearly to a schoolmaster forever two thirds of the rents of the said land to teach such a number of poor children as the minister and vestry of the said parish can with him agree." John Allen appointed as executors of his will Colonel Henry Fitzhugh, Major John Fitzhugh and the Reverend David Stuart, and by deeds dated the 9th of March 1725/6 and the 11th of June 1728 they purchased land in Stafford County for the purposes mentioned in the will of their testator.

It appears likely that John Allen was an intimate friend of the Reverend David Stuart as to his son William Stuart, then not yet two years of age, he bequeathed three thousand pounds of tobacco.

Upon the lands bequeathed to the parish by John Allen the second church of

Saint Paul's was built. A frame building, it apparently stood near the present brick edifice. Since the Reverend David Stuart arrived in the parish about 1722 and seemingly gave new inspiration to the parishioners it is believed that the second church was erected shortly after 1725. Some strength is lent to this assumption by the gift of a very handsome flagon, chalice and paten which bear hallmarks indicating they were made in London in 1720 and thus engraved:

> "Given by Henry Fitzhugh of Stafford County,
> St. Paul's Parish, Gent: for ye use of ye
> Church"

These articles are yet in use at Saint Paul's Church and it is likely that they were presented shortly after the new church was occupied. The donor, Colonel Henry Fitzhugh (1686/7-1758), was the son of Colonel William Fitzhugh (1651-1701).

The church also has another handsome silver chalice which is engraved as follows:

> "PRESENTED
> TO
> The Rev. William Friend
> By
> The Ladies of the Congregation
> of St. Paul's Church
> King George CQ Virginia
> 1859"

Other engraved brass memorial pieces furnish and adorn the alter, however these are all of the present Century.

Of the early ministers of Saint Paul's Parish we have no reliable account until the Reverend David Stuart took charge about 1722. We may infer that the Reverend Giles Rainsford preceeded him, since he is mentioned in the Bible record of Colonel Henry Fitzhugh of "Bedford." Fitzhugh's first child to be baptized was Ann Fitzhugh, who was born the 8th of March 1720/1 and her father records she was baptized by the Rev. Mr. Giles Ranceford [Rainsford]. Just following this entry is that of the birth of the Colonel's next child, Henry Fitzhugh, on the 18th of September 1723; we note that he was baptized by the Reverend Mr. David Stuart. It appears that all the other children of Colonel Henry Fitzhugh (1686/7-1758) of "Bedford" and his wife nee Susanna Cooke (1693-1749) were baptized by the Reverend David Stuart; thus it is obvious that Rainsford's tenure was of short duration. (For some years prior to 1719 the Reverend Mr. Rainsford had been rector of Saint Anne's Parish, Essex County, but about that time, for reasons not exactly clear, he had been replaced by the Reverend John Bagge, by the order of Colonel Alexander Spotswood (1676-1740), then Governor of Virginia. Though the vestry of Saint Anne's Parish protested the removal, they were forced to accept the Reverend John Bagge after the Governor directed a very heated letter to them. After his short term as minister at Saint Paul's Parish, the Reverend Mr. Rainsford removed to Maryland).

The Reverend David Stuart officiated as rector of Saint Paul's Parish from 1722 until the time of his death on the 31st of January 1748/9 after a short illness. He was followed in this charge by his eldest son the Reverend William Stuart and we are principally indebted to these two gentlemen for the entries in Saint Paul's Parish Register. They devoted their lives to their ecclesiastical duties and many of their descendants have through the years been devoted communicants of Saint Paul's Parish.

The Reverend David Stuart was born at Inverness, Scotland; he served under the Pretender, Prince James, in 1715 and fled to Virginia in that year. He went to England for Holy Orders and tradition has it returned to Virginia by way of Barbadoes, marrying there Jane Gibbons, daughter of William Gibbons, Esquire. Upon reaching Virginia he immediately took charge of Saint Paul's Parish where his eldest child, William Stuart, was born the 13th of December 1723. Reverend David Stuart acquired considerable landed estate in the counties of Stafford, Westmoreland, Fauquier, Fairfax and Prince William. This landed estate, together with a handsome personal estate, left his children in excellent financial situations and they married into prominent Virginia families.

It would seem that the new minister and his bride were not without acquaintances in Stafford County. Tradition has it that Mrs. Stuart was the younger sister of the wife of the Reverend Alexander Scott (1686-1738) who was minister of Overwharton Parish 1711-1738. This divine is known to have married Sarah (Gibbons Brent (1693-1733), daughter of William Gibbons, Esquire, of Wiltshire, and widow c William Brent, Esquire, (circa 1677-1709) of "Richland" in Overwharton Parish, Sta ford County, Virginia, by whom he had no issue. William Brent went to England to claim the estate of Stoke and Admington in Gloucestershire and married there the aforementioned Sarah Gibbons on the 12th of May 1709 and died on the 26th of November 1709 in Middlesex, England, leaving his wife enceinte, and their son William Brent (1710-1742) was born the 6th of March following his father's death. When he was seven, his widowed mother brought him to Stafford County to claim the vaste estates to which he was entitled as the only surviving male heir of his great gran father Colonel Giles Brent of Maryland and Virginia. Sarah (Gibbons) Brent was married secondly on the 20th of May 1717 to the Reverend Alexander Scott, minister of Overwharton Parish, and their handsome tombstones now repose in Aquia Churchyard. The last mentioned William Brent (1710-1742) married Jane (surname unknown) and we find the births and baptisms of their two only children recorded in Saint Paul's Parish Register by the Reverend David Stuart. Doctor Richard Henry Stuart (1808-1889) of "Cedar Grove" was mindful of his kinship to the Brents of "Richland" when upon inquiry from his cousin, Mr. Robert T. Knox of Fredericksburg, Virginia, in 1877, he wrote him that this relationship came about by a sister of his great grandmother Stuart, nee Jane Gibbons, marrying "Mr. Brent of Richland." Thus we see that the Reverend Alexander Scott, rector of Overwharton Parish 1711-1738, and the Reverend David Stuart, rector of Saint Paul's Parish 1722-1749, were brothers-in-law, and as the former was the senior of the latter it may well be that the Reverend Alexander Scott was instrumental in the Reverend David Stuart being assig ed to Saint Paul's Parish.

The Reverend William Stuart was educated at the College of William and Mary in Williamsburg and subsequently studied theology in England where he was ordained and licensed for Virginia the 26th of September 1746. He received the King's Boun ty on the 8th of October 1746 and returned to Virginia. He was assigned as minist er of South Farnham Parish, Essex County, and held that charge 1747-1749. After th death of his father, the Reverend David Stuart on the 31st of January 1748/9, he came to Saint Paul's Parish. He was noted for his eloquence in the pulpit and for his popularity among his parishioners. Of him a granddaughter has written: "'Parson Stuart', as he was called, was held in high esteem. His pure, moral and religious character, high toned integrity, liberal education, and courteous genial deportment commanded the sincere regard and revential respect of that gay, frolic loving but generous, noble hearted people."

Reverend William Stuart served Saint Paul's Parish until ill health forced him to resign in 1796. His letter of resignation is most touching:

> "To the Vestry of St. Paul's Parish
> "Gentlemen:
> "I have been curate of this parish upward of forty years. My own conscience bears me witness, and I trust my parishioners (though many of them have fallen asleep) will also witness, that until age and infirmities disabled me I always, so far as my infirmities would allow, faithfully discharged my duties as a minister of the Gospel. It has given me many hours of anxious concern that the services of the Church should be so long discontinued on my account. The spirit indeed is willing, but the flesh is weak. I therefore entreat the favour of you to provide me a successor as soon as you can, that divine service may be discontinued no longer; and at the end of the year the glebe shall be given up to him by your affectionate servant,
>
> William Stuart"

The vestry accepted the resignation of their beloved minister on the 19th of January 1797. The Reverend William Stuart died at his plantation "Cedar Grove" on the 1st of October 1798 "after a tedious confinement with the Gout" as is recorded in Saint Paul's Parish Register in the handwriting of his son, Richard Stuart, Esquire, (1770-1835), who succeeded him at that seat.

The Reverend William Stuart was married on the 26th of November 1750 to Sarah Foote who was born the 29th of January 1732/3, daughter of Richard Foote, Gentleman; he presented the young couple as a wedding gift that valuable estate lying between Chotank Creek and Potomac River called "Cedar Grove." The original Stuart residence was destroyed by fire shortly after the death of Richard Stuart (1770-1835) and the present brick mansion erected about 1840 by his son, Doctor Richard Henry Stuart (1808-1889), who resided there until his death.

Richard Stuart married on the 28th of July 1802 Mrs. Margaret (Robinson) McCarty (1780-1808), widow of Daniel McCarty of "Longwood," Westmoreland County, and daughter of William and Margaret (Williamson) Robinson, and thereby allied himself to families long established in the parish. Richard Stuart, by his said marriage, became the step-father of two little girls, left motherless at tender years to whom he was much attached, viz: (1) Anne Robinson McCarty, born the 28th of September 1798, who married Major Henry Lee of "Stratford"; and (2) Elizabeth McCarty, born the 9th of November 1800, mistress of "Stratford" for more than fifty years, who married Henry D. Storke of Leedstown, Westmoreland County. During the long term of Mrs. Storke's residence at "Stratford" and the Stuarts at "Cedar Grove," for whom she displayed much affection, there are preserved letters which give evidence of this long and amiable assocation. Upon her death in 1879 Mrs. Storke bequeathed "Stratford" to her two great nephews, Judge Charles E. Stuart and Dr. Richard H. Stuart, and in 1929 their heirs sold the estate to the Robert E. Lee Memorial Foundation, Incorporated.

Doctor Richard Henry Stuart (1808-1889), only son of Richard and Margaret (Robinson) Stuart, married on the 7th of May 1833 at "Riversdale," Prince George's County, Maryland, Julia Calvert (1814-1888), daughter of George Calvert, Esquire, (1768-1838), builder of that elegant mansion which is now owned by The Maryland-National Capital Park and Planning Commission. George Calvert's sister Eleanor Calvert (1758-1811) married first in 1774 Colonel John Parke Custis (1755-1781), only son to survive infancy of Colonel Daniel Parke Custis (1711-1757) of New Kent County and his wife nee Martha Dandridge (1731-1802) who married secondly, in 1759, Colonel George Washington (1732-1799). The only son of Colonel John Parke and Eleanor (Calvert) Custis was George Washington Parke Custis (1781-1857), builder of "Arlington," who was a first cousin of the abovementioned Julia (Calvert) Stuart, and she was a bridesmaid on the 30th of April 1831 at "Arlington" when Mary Ann Randolph Custis (1808-1873), only child of George Washington Parke Custis (1781-1857) and his wife nee Mary Lee Fitzhugh (1788-1853) married Lieutenant Robert Edward Lee (1807-1870), son of General Henry Lee and his second wife Ann Hill Carter. Thus, Mrs. Stuart of "Cedar Grove" and Mrs. Lee of "Arlington" were descendants of the Honorable George Calvert (1579-1632), First Lord Baltimore, Proprietor of Maryland, and were intimate life-time friends. Furthermore Doctor Richard Henry Stuart's uncle, Doctor David Stuart (1753-1815) of "Hope Park," Fairfax County, Virginia, had married in 1783 the abovementioned Eleanor (Calvert) Custis, widow of Colonel John Parke Custis. Doctor David Stuart, one of the first three Commissioners of the District of Columbia, was a particular favorite of General Washington and mentioned in his last will and Testament.

The close kinship and association of the Custises and Lees of "Arlington" and the Stuarts of "Cedar Grove" is indicated by surviving documents. In 1855 Agnes Lee (1841-1873), daughter of General Robert E. Lee, wrote an account of a delightful visit to her cousins at "Cedar Grove" as well as other places in Saint Paul's Parish.

Doctor Richard Henry Stuart and his wife nee Julia Calvert left no surviving son; "Cedar Grove" passed to their daughter Rosalie Eugenia Stuart (1835-1915) who married her cousin Sholto Turberville Stuart (1821-1884). He was the son of Charles Calvert Stuart (1794-1846) of "Chantilly," Fairfax County, and his wife nee Cornelia Lee Turberville (1797-1883), and grandson of Doctor David Stuart and his wife nee Eleanor Custis, above mentioned.

Remembering his close kinship and association with the Stuarts of "Cedar Grove," Captain Robert Edward Lee (1843-1916), son of the great Southern Chieftain, shortly after his second marriage to Juliet Carter, wrote his cousin Mrs. Sholto Turberville Stuart at "Cedar Grove" from his home in Washington, D.C., on the 2nd of October 1895, as follows:

......"If you would like to have us, my wife and I want to

pay you a visit of a day or two this month.

"We are going to take a drive in a one horse buggy
down through your country to visit Stratford and the other
Lee places in the Northern Neck. We start from Ravensworth
[the Fitzhugh - Lee estate in Fairfax County], go to Fredericksburg, stay there with Dan Lee a day or two and then
make Cedar Grove and from there to Stratford, Chantilly,
Lee Hall, Cobbs Hall, Ditchley, Corotoman, Sabine Hall &c.
This is our plan now. As you know we can not always carry
out these plans. What I want you to write me is whether it
will be perfectly convenient for you to have us.

"We are very plain people and are coming to see you
and Cedar Grove and all your children. I want to show my
wife the place where I spent so many happy hours in my boy-
hood, and introduce her to the many sweet cousins. But we
both know how different things are in Virginia now and
want you to tell us whether it is perfectly convenient for
you to have us."

Captain Lee had many pleasant memories of ante-bellum days in Saint Paul's
Parish and, if his visit fell on a Sunday, doubtless attended divine services at
Saint Paul's Church. The edifice of his time, still standing, took the place of
the early Eighteenth Century frame structure.

It appears in 1762 the vestry of Saint Paul's Parish decided to replace the
frame church and the Virginia Gazette of the 12th of February 1762 carried an
advertisement requesting bids for the construction of "a commodious Brick Church
in St. Paul's Parish, Stafford County." This was signed by John Stith and William Fitzhugh, church wardens. No further action appears to have been taken by
the parish vestry until the 18th of July 1766 when the following more detailed
notice appeared in the Virginia Gazette:

"To be Let to the lowest bidder on Friday, the 29th of
August, The building of a Brick Church in Saint Paul's Parish,
Stafford County, in the form of a Cross, of the following Dimensions, each wing to be 16 feet in clear of the length and 26 feet
in breadth, 2 feet high to the water table and 24 to the ceiling,
with three galleries.

"Any person inclining to undertake the same, are desired to
meet at the Church of the said Parish at the time above mentioned.
Five hundred pounds will be paid in hand, the undertaker giving
Bond with sufficient security for the faithful performance of the
said Building.

                                        S. Washington)
                                        W. Fitzhugh)Church Wardens"

The above dimensions would produce a building in the form of a Greek cross,
fifty eight by fifty eight feet in the clear (i.e., inside the upper walls), and
and the presently existing Saint Paul's Church is practically identical with
these specifications except that the wings of the edifice are about three inches
narrower than specified. The upper walls of the present building are about two
feet thick and are laid in Flemish bond without glazed headers.

SAINT PAUL'S PARISH

In accordance with the prevailing style in Virginia church architecture at the time Saint Paul's Church was built, the existing building has two tiers of windows, the upper row serving to give light and air to the three galleries which occupied all the wings of the church except the east one, in which the chancel was located. A central doorway, evidently of classic pedimented type, was provided at the west end of the nave and a similiar one at each end of the north-and-south transept. The roof is hipped at the end of each wing, but the original location of the pulpit is not known.

The Reverend William Stuart must have been very proud of the new brick church and presented a large and handsomely bound Bible which yet rests on the high pulpit. It was restored a few years ago by the donor's great-great-granddaughter, Mrs. Benjamin Custis Grymes (nee Rosalie Stuart). The Bible was printed in 1762 by Joseph Bentham, printer to the University of Cambridge, and "Sold by Benjamin Dod, Bookseller, at the Bible & Key in Ave - Mary Lane, near St. Paul's, London." The original binding is embellish in gold lettering on the front:

> "GIVEN FOR THE USE
> OF THE CHURCH IN
> ST. PAUL'S PARISH
> BY THE REV.^D WILLIAM
> STUART, RECTOR OF
> THE SAID PARISH
> 1769"

Shortly after the new brick church was completed George Washington twice attended divine services at Saint Paul's Church; he enters the dates in his diary as the 29th of May 1768 and the 4th of September 1768. He was visiting his brother Colonel Samuel Washington (1734-1781), a vestryman in Saint Paul's Parish. Samuel Washington lived on an estate inherited from his father, Captain Augustine Washington (1694-1743), and had many relatives there. Captain Augustine Washington, left an orphan by the deaths of his parents, was raised in Saint Paul's Parish by his paternal relatives; when but three years of age he received a legacy from his great-aunt Madam Martha (Washington) Hayward (circa 1643-1697), widow of Samuel Hayward, Gentleman, who with his brother Mr. Nicholas Hayward of London, have been previously mentioned as benefactors of Chotank Parish. Colonel Samuel Washington sold his estate in Saint Paul's Parish about 1772 to Colonel Henry Fitzhugh of "Bedford" and moved to "Harewood," Jefferson County, now West Virginia, where he died. George Washington often visited his relatives in Saint Paul's Parish before and after his brother's residence there; as a boy he was presumably visiting his relatives "in the Chotank" when his father was taken ill at the family home, "Ferry Farm," and a messenger was dispatched to bring him home. The earliest known examples of George Washington's boyish signature appear on the title page of a volume that once belonged to Captain Samuel Bowman (1681-1742), mariner, whose handsome tombstone is in the cemetery at "Eagle's Nest," the estate long in the possession of Colonel William Fitzhugh (1651-1701) and the descendants of his eldest son Colonel William Fitzhugh (circa 1677-1713). Here too is the crumbling tomb of the latter's wife, nee Ann Lee (1683-1731/2), daughter of the Honorable Richard Lee, who married secondly Captain Daniel McCarty (1679-1724) of Cople Parish, Westmoreland County. The death of Madam Ann (Lee) Fitzhugh McCarty is recorded in Saint Paul's Parish Register.

SAINT PAUL'S PARISH

Recalling his long and amiable association among his cousins in Saint Paul's Parish, General Washington by his last will and Testament bequeathed "to the acquaintances and friends of my juvenile years, Lawrence Washington and Robert Washington, of Chotank, two gold headed canes, having my Arms engraved upon them and to each a spyglass as they will be useful where they live." These men, Lawrence Washington (1728-circa 1814) of "Waterloo" and Robert Washington (1730-circa 1800 of "Woodstock" both in Saint Paul's Parish, were distant cousins of General Washington (1732-1799) and survived him. The gold headed cane and spyglass bequeathed to Lawrence Washington are now at "Mount Vernon," while the spyglass bequeathed to Robert Washington is believed to be identical with the one engraved by its maker "J.Gilbert, Tower Hill, London," and now in possession of descendants of the Washington family in Saint Paul's Parish.

After the death of the Reverend William Stuart in 1798, the early part of the Nineteenth Century witnessed a general decline of Episcopalism throughout Virginia. Many of its handsome colonial churchs fell to decay. Saint Paul's was saved, at least in basic architecture, by conversion to a county academy in 1813. The colonial interior, however, suffered severely. All woodwork was torn out; various partitions were installed, as well as a second floor; the north and west entrance doorways were closed with brickwork, and other alterations made to suit its new use. The academy proved unsuccessful. Happily, a petition to the state legislature restored the building to the parish in 1831 and the structure was again consecrated as Saint Paul's Church by Bishop Richard Channing Moore on the 15th of May 1831. Unfortunately, in the remodelling which took place at this time, no attempt was made to restore the colonial arrangement of the building.

Though the old church stands as a monument to colonial days, the parish of Saint Paul's was destined to become a part of another county when the church was yet new, and at the same time its bounds, which had remained unaltered during the colonial period, were to be enlarged.

Various petitions were received by the House of Burgesses beginning in 1769 "for a new modelling of the counties of Richmond, Westmoreland, King George and Stafford." Finally on the 3rd of June 1775 the House of Burgesses ordered "that leave be given to bring in a bill for altering and establishing the boundries of the counties of King George and Stafford and Mr. Jones, Mr. Fitzhugh, and Mr. Charles Carter of Stafford, do prepare and bring in the same." The Honorable Joseph Jones (1727-1805) of "Spring Hill" and the Honorable William Fitzhugh of "Chatham" represented King George County, while Colonel Charles Carter (1733-1796) of "Ludlow" represented Stafford County. Judge Joseph Jones presented the bill to the House and the Council shortly concurred but before the bill was signed, the Honorable John Murray, Earl of Dunmore, lieutenant governor of Virginia, fled from Williamsburg and took refauge on a British man-of-war and the Royal Government in Virginia was dissolved; the Revolution had begun. However, on the 15th of October 1776 the bill was again presented to the legislators assembled at Williamsburg and that assembly ordered extensive alterations in the boundries of King George and Stafford counties to be effective the 1st of January 1777.

Since the formation of Stafford and King George counties the upper or western section of the Northern Neck penisula had been about equally divided between

SAINT PAUL'S PARISH

the westward extensions of Westmoreland County on the Potomac River and Richmond
County on the Rappahannock River. Thus the counties of Stafford [formed from
Westmoreland County in 1664] and King George [formed from Richmond County in
1721] were long and narrow and were divided by the natural ridge of the Northern
Neck, that is to say, that territory which was drained by the Potomac River was
Stafford County and that territory which was drained by the Rappahannock River
was King George County. A more convenient division of Stafford and King George
counties was effected by the Act of 1776. This directed that the two counties
be divided about the middle across the Northern Neck peninsula, beginning at the
mouth of Muddy Creek on the Rappahannock River and following it upstream to its
headwaters near where present Route 218 crosses it and thence in a straight line
[which presently divides the farms of Mrs. Thomas Benton Gayle, Senior, and her
son Robert L. Gayle] to the head spring of Whipsewasin [Whipewaughson] Creek,
and thence down the meanders of the said creek to its junction with Potomac Creek
and thence down this creek to Potomac River.

By this approximately North-South division of the two counties, the lower
portion of Stafford County along the Potomac River was given to King George County and the upper portion of King George County along the Rappahannock River was
given to Stafford County. The entire bounds of colonial Saint Paul's Parish fell
into King George County.

So, during the first three score years the records in the Register of Saint
Paul's Parish pertain mostly to residents of Stafford County; for the last score
mostly to residents of King George County. Thus the court records of both counties must be consulted by anyone attempting to trace families domiciled in Saint
Paul's Parish. The Westmoreland County court records are oftentimes helpful.

Because of the meanderings of Machodoc Creek, the colonial southern boundry
of Saint Paul's Parish, the neck of land north of Rosier's Creek [called Machodoc
Neck], which was during the colonial period in Washington Parish, Westmoreland
County, jutted far into Saint Paul's Parish and a neck of land in lower Saint
Paul's Parish [commonly called Pumpkin Neck] jutted into Washington Parish. Across Machodoc Creek was constantly kept "the Little Ferry" and thus there was
considerable intercourse between families residing in Saint Paul's Parish and
upper Washington Parish and we find quite a few entries in Saint Paul's Parish
Register concerning inhabitants of Washington Parish.

By another alteration in county boundry lines, that portion of Washington
Parish, Westmoreland County, north of Rosier's Creek was added to King George
County in 1779, and thus Machodoc Neck and adjacent lands became a part of Saint
Paul's Parish, King George County. Washington Parish was without a regular minister from the beginning of the Revolutionary War until many years thereafter;
since the Reverend William Stuart was nearby it is natural enough to find many
people in the area between Machodoc and Rosier's Creek included in his entries
of marriages in Saint Paul's Parish Register.

About the time the Reverend David Stuart became minister of Saint Paul's
Parish, "Round Hill," the upper church of Washington Parish was rebuilt of brick
and completed in 1722. It stood not far from the present post office of Tetotum
and near the gate to the "Spy Hill" estate. The Reverend Roderick McCulloch,

SAINT PAUL'S PARISH

rector of Washington Parish during 1731-1745, is said to have baptized the infant George Washington on the 5th of April 1732. Reverend David Stuart officiated at the marriage of the Reverend Mr. McCulloch on the 17th of February 1734/5 to Elizabeth Weedon. The Reverend William Stuart married the next known minister of Washington Parish, the Reverend Mr. Archibald Campbell, to his first wife Rebecca Rallings on the 15th of January 1753. Reverend Archibald Campbell was rector of Washington Parish 1745-1775; the massive tombstone of his first wife is the sole remaining object on the site of pre-Revolutionary Round Hill Episcopal Church. The tomb reads:

"Here is buried
Mrs. Rebeckah Campbell
wife of
Reverend Mr. Archibald Campbell
Minister of Washington Parish.
She died the XXI of March MDCCLIV
in the XX year of her age.
Here also lies Alexander, their child".

The interrelations of Saint Paul's, Overwharton and Washington parishes fascinate the genealogist and tell the general student a great deal about colonial life. It would be a source of greater instruction if complete records of all the parishes and counties existed. It is indeed fortunate that the Register of Saint Paul's Parish exists and has been scientifically preserved; it does much to advance our knowledge of persons in all three parishes.

A study of Saint Paul's Parish Register shows that both the Reverend David Stuart and the Reverend William Stuart married many parties who were not residents of their parish; among these were Thomas Chancellor and Katherine Cooper, daughter of Doctor John Cooper, all of Washington Parish, Westmoreland County, who were married by the Reverend David Stuart on the 3rd of March 1723/4. They were the great-great-great-great-great-grandparents of this compiler. The discovery of that entry spurred my genealogical interest when I was yet in my 'teens, and the Register's then crumbling pages yielded other data of great genealogical interest to me. My hope is that others, through the arrangement here presented, will find items of interest - and if they do, it will be with considerable less effort than it has been for me.

And now as I write on the porch of my summer cottage in Saint Paul's Parish, my eyes wander out over the placid waters of the Potomac River and I reflect upon that spring day in June 1608 when Captain John Smith and a little band of explorers sailed by the great forests which then covered these banks. Up the Potomac a bit from my cottage I can see the mouth of Passapatanzy Creek and beyond the bays formed by Potomac Creek and Aquia Creek emptying their waters into the big estuary. At the conflux of Potomac Creek and Potomac River is Marlborough Point, site of the King of Potomac's tribal capital, which was visited some years after Captain Smith's exploration by the Indian Princess Pocahontas and my ancestor Captain Raleigh Croshaw, Gentleman, who came to Jamestown in the Second Supply the latter part of September 1608. Here the Potomac makes almost a right angle turn to the northward and at night, at a distance of about ten miles, we can see the lights of the Marine Corps Base at Quantico, Virginia, and beyond the haze

cast by the lights of the City of Washington. Down the river lie the planta-
tions of the Washingtons, the Lees, the Monroes and many other founders of this
now vast nation. From Jamestown westward, through Saint Paul's Parish and beyond, the founding fathers brought with them the word of God and the ideals of
Anglo-Saxon liberty.

George H.S. King

Saint Paul's Parish,
King George County, Virginia,
1st of August 1960.

MEMORIAL TABLETS IN SAINT PAUL'S CHURCH

* * *

IN MEMORY
of
JUDITH BLACKBURN
Wife of
Gustavus B. Alexander
Died April 6th 1866
Aged 68 years.

Blessed are the dead which #
die in the Lord. Rev.xiv : 13 #

* * *
* *
*

TO THE GLORY OF GOD
IN MEMORY OF
JOSEPH RAPHAEL ANDRUS
Missionary to Africa
First Rector of this Parish
after its Revival
1817 - 1820
First Missionary of the
Protestant Episcopal Church in Va.
to a Foreign Land
January 1821
Born in Cornwall, Vt., April 3rd 1791
Ordained by Bishop Griswold
of the Eastern Diocese
Died in Africa, July 28, 1821.

————

This tablet erected by the
Diocese of Virginia
1935

* * *
* *
*

————————————

#In the church cemetery is a tombstone in memory of Gustavus Brown Alexander
(1793-1860) of "Caledon", Saint Paul's Parish, and his wives, Sarah Blair Stuart
(1802-1833) and Judith Ball Backburn (1799-1866).

MEMORIAL TABLETS IN SAINT PAUL'S CHURCH

DAVID STUART
Became the minister of St. Paul's Parish
King George County in 1722.
He continued as the minister of this
parish until his death in 1749.
WILLIAM STUART
Son of David, was ordained, and licensed by
the Bishop of London for service in Va.
in September 1746. He became the minister
of St. Paul's Parish in 1749,
upon the death of his father, and held
the charge until 1790* when he resigned
on account of ill health. He died in 1796.#

— — —

DESCENDANTS AND FAITHFUL MEMBERS
OF THIS CHURCH

Sept.4,1770	Richard Stuart	March 1835
	His wife	
1780	Margaret Robinson	1808
May 31,1808	Dr.Richard H.Stuart	May 14,1889
	His wife	
Jan.31,1814	Julia Calvert	June 8, 1889*#
1835	Rosalie S. Stuart	1915
1867	Richard H. Stuart	1925
1875	George C. Stuart	1949

* * *
* *
*

---

*   The date 1790 is an error; the Reverend William Stuart was minister 1749-1796.

\#   The date 1796 is an error; the Reverend William Stuart was born the 13th of December 1723 and died the 1st of October 1798, aged seventy five years, both in Saint Paul's Parish and agreeable to recordings in the Register thereof.

*# The date 1889 is an error; Mrs.Julia (Calvert) Stuart died June 8, 1888.

VESTRYMEN OF SAINT PAUL'S PARISH

1720 - 1857

The Eighteenth Century vestry books of Saint Paul's Parish have been lost.
It appears, however, that Bishop William Meade (1789-1862) author of Old Churches,
Ministers and Families of Virginia (1857) had access to certain records not now
available and he gives a list of vestryman from the year 1720 to the present time
in his above cited work [Volume II, page 192], which is as follows:

Richard Bernard, John Hooe, Richard Foote, Captain John Alexander, Captain
Baldwin Dade, Colonel Henry Fitzhugh, Jerard [Gerard] Fowke, John Stith, Cadwal-
lader Dade, John Stewart [Stuart], John Alexander, Jr., Francis Thornton, John
Washington, Thomas Pratt, Thomas Bunbury, (Thomas Stribling, reader,), Henry
Fitzhugh,Jr., William Fitzhugh, William Fitzhugh, Jr.,[1] Samuel Washington[2],
Laurence Washington, Townsend Dade, in the place of Samuel Washington, who remov-
ed in 1770; John Berryman, in 1771, in place of William Fitzhugh[1], who removed
out of the county; Robert Washington, Andrew Grant, Robert Stith, W.G. Stuart,
William Hooe, Daniel Fitzhugh, William Thornton, William Stith, Henry Fitzhugh,
Robert Yates, William Storke, William Quarles, Thomas Short, Benjamin Grymes,
Thomas Washington, Rice W. Hooe, John B. Fitzhugh, John Waugh, Langhorne Dade,
William Stone, Henry A. Ashton, Charles Stuart, J.K. Washington, Abraham B. Hooe,
J.J.Stuart, William F. Grymes, Charles Massey, J. Quesenbury, Robert Chesley,
Needam Washington, Alexander Keech, Francis C. Fitzhugh, B.O. Tayloe, Thomas
Smith, Dr. Robert Parsons, Gustavus B. Alexander, Henry Maustin, Hezekiah Potts,
T.L. Lomax, Jacob W. Stuart, Henry T. Washington, Drury B. Fitzhugh, Benjamin R.
Grymes, John T. Washington, W.E. Stuart, M. Tenent.

Bishop Meade states that the earlier part of his mother's life was spent in
Saint Paul's Parish under the ministry of the Reverend William Stuart and he has
often heard her "speak in high praise of him." His mother, nee Mary Grymes (November 9, 1753 - June 16, 1813), was the only daughter of Benjamin Grymes, Senior,
Esquire, and his first wife Betty Fitzhugh, daughter of Colonel Henry Fitzhugh
(circa 1706-1742) of "Eagle's Nest" and Lucy Carter, his wife. She was married,
first on the 18th of May 1770 in Saint Paul's Parish by the Reverend William Stuart,
to William Randolph, and secondly on the 10th of December 1780 to General Richard
Kidder Meade (July 14, 1746 - February 9, 1805) of "Lucky Hit," Clark County, Va.,
and Bishop Meade was one of their several children. He was, therefore, closely
connected to Saint Paul's Parish and has left us an excellent account in his above
cited work.

---

1 - Note the differentiation between William Fitzhugh (1725-1791) of "Marmion"
    and his younger cousin William Fitzhugh (1741-1809) who is called "junior"
    while they both resided in Saint Paul's Parish. Though he retained possess-
    ion of his estates "Eagle's Nest" and "Somerset" in Saint Paul's Parish his
    entire life, after building "Chatham" about 1769,William Fitzhugh [Jr.] lived
    there and was consequently replaced on the vestry as the above record indicates.
2 - Colonel Samuel Washington (1734-1781) removed to Jefferson County, Virginia.

A

B. Susannah, daughter of Philip and Mary Ackinson, September 27, 1715.

M. John Acres and Dully Griffin, May 28, 1790.

M. Mary Adams and George Elliot, April 26, 1728.

D. William Adams, October 28, 1735.

M. Thomas Adams and Katherine Skinner, October 18, 1738.

M. Margaret Addason and John Sweney, October 6, 1769.

M. John Addison and Mary Ann Findleston, April 17, 1761.

B. Anne, daughter of John and Mary Anne Addison, February 4, 1762.

B. William, son of John and Mary Ann Addison, June 5, 1764.

B. Verlinda, daughter of John and Mary Addison, October 8, 1764 [? 1765].

B. Sarah, daughter of John and Mary Anne Addison, August 13, 1767.

B. James, son of John and Mary Anne Addison, July 6, 1769.

M. John Addison and Monica Bryant, March 19, 1789.

M. Sarah Addison and John Watson, February 27, 1790.

D. Philip Adkison, January 12, 1735/6.

D. Elizabeth Adrington, December 4, 1725.

D. Francis Adrington, December 4, 1725.

D. Helen Aisom, April 2, 1726.

B. Frances Anne, daughter of Jane Alderton, September 5, 1735.

M. Philip Alexander and Sarah Hooe, November 11, 1726.

M. Anne Alexander and John Hooe, November 23, 1726.

B. Frances, daughter of Philip and Sarah Alexander, October 5, 1728.

B. Jane, daughter of Philip and Sarah Alexander, January 12, 1729/30.

B. Elizabeth, daughter of Philip and Sarah Alexander, December 24, 1731.

1

M. Parthenia Alexander and Dade Massey, January 17, 1731/2.

B. Sarah, daughter of Philip and Sarah Alexander, September 30, 1733.

M. John Alexander and Susanna Pearson, December 15, 1734.

D. Major Robert Alexander, October 5, 1735.

B. John, son of Philip and Sarah Alexander, November 13, 1735.

D. Elizabeth Alexander, March 23, 1735/6.

M. Sarah Alexander and Baldwin Dade, August 7, 1736.

B. Charles, son of John and Susanna Alexander, July 20, 1737.

D. Mrs. Anne Alexander, September 23, 1739.

B. John, son of John and Susanna Alexander, January 15, 1739/40.

B. Philip, son of Philip and Sarah Alexander, May 31, 1741.

B. Anne, daughter of John and Susanna Alexander, February 9, 1741/2.

B. William, son of Captain Philip and Sarah Alexander, March 3, 1743/4.

B. Susanna, daughter of John and Susanna Alexander, April 12, 1744.

B. Gerard, son of John and Susanna Alexander, June 13, 1746.

B. Robert, son of Philip and Sarah Alexander, August 2, 1746.

B. Simon Pearson, son of Captain John and Susanna Alexander, January 20, 1747/8.

M. Jane Alexander and Henry Ashton, February 23, 1748/9.

M. Frances Alexander and John Stuart, February 16, 1749/50.

M. Sarah Alexander and John Fendall, September 24, 1751.

B. Mary, daughter of John and Lucy Alexander, November 26, 1756.

B. Lucy, daughter of John and Lucy Alexander, December 4, 1757.

B. William, son of John and Susanna Alexander, April 29, 1758.

B. Sarah, daughter of John and Lucy Alexander, November 17, 1758.

M. Anne Alexander and Charles Binns, October 4, 1759

B. Philip Thornton, son of John and Lucy Alexander, October 14, 1760.

B. Frances, daughter of John and Lucy Alexander, August 24, 1762.

B. Alice, daughter of John and Lucy Alexander, June 20, 1764.

M. William Alexander and Sigismunda Mary Massey, April 18, 1765.

M. Susanna Alexander and Pearson Chapman, July 31, 1766.

B. William Thornton, son of John and Lucy Alexander, June 28, 1768.

M. Mary Alexander and George Thornton, October 9, 1773.

M. Lucy Alexander and John Taliaferro, January 24, 1774.

M. Sarah Alexander and Seymour Hooe, March 9, 1776.

M. Lucy Alexander and William Quarles, October 20, 1784.

M. John Alias and Mary Oneal, September 17, 1722.

M. William Allason and Anne Hooe, June 26, 1772.

ALLEN : ALLAN

B. Ann, daughter of Archibald and Sarah Allen, December 17, 1717.

D. James Allen, April 11, 1720.

B. Mary, daughter of Archibald and Sarah Allen, October 2, 1721.

D. Sarah, wife of Archibald Allen, November 12, 1721.

M. Archibald Allan and Penelope Skinner, December 26, 1722.

D. John Allan, October 14, 1725.

M. Francis Allan and Katherine Campbell, November 17, 1747.

M. Andrew Allen and Alice Sebastian, February 12, 1750/1.

M. Richard Allen and Nancy Jones, February 4, 1788.

ALLENTHROPE : ALLENTRAP : ALINTRAP   SEE: YARENTHARP [Page 157]

M. John Allenthrope and Anne Sebastian, April 16, 1723.

B. Anne, daughter of John and Anne Allenthrope, December 7, 1725.

B. Sarah, daughter of John and Anne Allantrap, April 2, 1728.

B. John, son of John and Anne Allenthrope, June 3, 1732.

B. Elizabeth, daughter of John and Elizabeth Alintrope, April 10, 1735.

B. Mildred, daughter of John and Mary Alintrap, June 8, 1738.

M. Jane Allerton and Robert Raddish, October 12, 1735.

B. Henry, son of Moses and Anne Allgood, March 23, 1774.

M. William Allison and Anne Fitzhugh, November 21, 1740.

B. Mary Anne, daughter of William and Anne Allison, October 17, 1741.

B. John, son of William and Anne Allison, January 21, 1742/3.

B. William, son of Doctor William and Anne Allison, June 6, 1744.

B. Henry, son of William and Anne Allison, September 10, 1745.

D. Mary Ann, daughter of Dr. William Allison, January 5, 1746/7.

D. Henry, son of Dr. William Allison, July 5, 1747.

M. John Alsop and Mary McDonald, August 20, 1737.

B. Edward, son of John and Mary Alsop, January 13, 1737/8.

M. John Alsop and Elizabeth Conway, December 30, 1739.

B. Mary, daughter of John and Elizabeth Alsop, March 26, 1741.

B. Elizabeth, daughter of John and Elizabeth Alsop, March 8, 1743/4.

B. Sarah, daughter of John and Elizabeth Alsop, June 17, 1747.

M. Elizabeth Alsop and William Jones, February 9, 1749/50.

M. Elizabeth Alsop and John Barret, May 25, 1760.

M. Robert Alsop and Elizabeth Mardus, January 3, 1791.

B. Thomas, son of William and Anne Ambrose, October 15, 1731.

AMBRY : AMBRIE   SEE: EMBRY : EMBRIE

B. Elizabeth, daughter of William and Anne Ambry, February 6, 1733/4.

B. Frances, daughter of William and Anne Ambry, March 3, 1735/6.

D. William Ambry, April 2, 1736.

M. Anne Ambrie and John Pavier, June 1, 1738.

M. Sarah Ambry and William Garrat, February 4, 1741/2.

M. Thomas Ammon and Sarah Edrington of Sittingbourne Parish, January 24, 1733/4.

ANCRAM : ANCROM : ANCRUM : ANCHRUM : ANKRUM

M. Mary Anchrum and John Smith, February 17, 1717/8.

M. John Ancrom and Mary Thomas, January 27, 1726/7.

M. Mary Ancrom and John Taylor, February 27, 1726/7.

B. Sarah, daughter of John and Mary Ancrum, November 23, 1727.

B. Katherine, daughter of John and Elizabeth Ancrum, September 30, 1731.

B. Frances, daughter of John and Mary Ancrum, February 3, 1733/4.

M. William Ankrum and Margaret Colvin, December 24, 1734.

D. William Ancram, January 6, 1734/5.

D. John Ancrum, January 1, 1735/6.

B. John, son of John and Mary Ancrum, August 3, 1736.

D. John Ancrum, January 12, 1736/7.

M. Mary Ancrum and George Bush, November 14, 1737.

M. Joel Ancrom and Verlinda Suttle, September 12, 1745.

M. Sarah Ancrum and Thomas Hawkins, July 13, 1746.

M. Mary Anderson and Martin Frayn, July 9, 1758.

M. Elizabeth Armour and James Thomson, August 10, 1724.

M. George Arnold and Sarah White of King George County, November 9, 1758.

M. Jemima Arnold and John Clift, December 26, 1777.

M. William Ashmore and Nancy Edrington, January 14, 1781.

M. Charles Ashton of Washington Parish and Sarah Butler of this Parish, September 22, 1733.

M. Henry Ashton and Jane Alexander, February 23, 1748/9.

M. Mary Ashton and Jacob Wray, May 13, 1761.

M. John Ashton and Elizabeth Jackson, May 16, 1766.

M. Lawrence Ashton and Elizabeth Ashton, April 19, 1768.

M. Lawrence Ashton and Hannah Gibbons Dade, February [blank], 1779.

M. Mary Watts Ashton and John Waugh, November 4, 1790.

B. Richard, son of Samuel and Mary Atwell, November 27, 1763.

B. Francis, son of Samuel and Mary Atwell, May 19, 1768.

M. Mary Atwell and Thomas Moss, September 10, 1772.

B. Samuel, son of Samuel and Mary Atwood, June 16, 1766.

                                  B

M. Benjamin Baber and Mildred Berry, November 10, 1791. [King George County
    Marriage Register records license issued for this couple May 11, 1790].

M. Barbara Bagg and Samuel Sandys, September 12, 1724.

M. Sarah Bagjah and Jethro Burnsplat, October 21, 1729.

M. John Baily and Sarah Frank of Washington Parish, January 6, 1745/6.

M. John Baker and Sarah Walker, October 30, 1725.

B. Thomas, son of John and Sarah Baker, January 19, 1726/7.

D. John Baker, June 26, 1728.

M. Winifred Baker of Westmoreland County and William Strother, September
    26, 1765.

B. Benjamin, son of Benjamin and Anne Ball, September 13, 1742.

B. Anne, daughter of Benjamin and Anne Ball, July 17, 1745.

B. Elizabeth, daughter of Benjamin and Anne Ball, October 4, 1747.

B. Susannah, daughter of Benjamin and Anne Ball, August 28, 1752.

B. James, son of Benjamin and Anne Ball, April 7, 1755.

M. Anne Ball and John Smith, December 26, 1765.

D. William Balltruph, March 1, 1719/20.

B. Nelly, daughter of William and Elizabeth Bankhead, May 15, 1777.

B. Alse, daughter of John and Mary Banton, June 20, 1716.

M. William Banton and Sarah Hamm, December 1, 1730.

B. Elizabeth, daughter of William and Sarah Banton, December 10, 1731.

B. John, son of William and Sarah Banton, March 10, 1733/3.

M. Robert Barber and Penelope Gorman, October 26, 1747.

M. James Barber and Susanna Dickerson, September 5, 1779.

M. Elizabeth Barker and John MacClanin, March 24, 1793.

B. William, son of Rehobeth and Julia Barnfather, May 19, 1717.

M. Frances Barnfather and John Wells, June 18, 1723.

M. Rehobeth Barnfather and Elizabeth Leg, December 31, 1724.

B. Henry, son of Henry and Elizabeth Barns, October 12, 1740.

M. Edward Barradall and Sarah Fitzhugh, January 5, 1735/6.

BARRETT : BARRET : BARRAT

B. Margaret and Helen, daughters of Richard and Margaret Barrett, April 19, 1728.

M. Richard Barret and Joyce Duncum, September 21, 1729.

B. William, son of Richard and Joyce Barrat, August 20, 1734.

B. Richard, son of Richard and Joyce Barret, March 19, 1737/8.

B. Anne, daughter of Elizabeth Barret, November 18, 1740.

B. Mary, daughter of Richard and Joyce Barret, September 21, 1741.

M. Joyce Barret and Joseph Clift, June 22, 1743.

B. Ketura, daughter of Sarah Barret, November 18, 1746.

M. John Barret and Elizabeth Alsop, May 25, 1760.

B. Richard, son of John and Elizabeth Barret, February 9, 1764.

B.   Anne Conway, daughter of John and Elizabeth Barrett, May 16, 1766.

B.   John, son of John and Elizabeth Barrett, March 9, 1768.

M.   William Barrett and Mary Hudson, December 30, 1785.

M.   Timothy Barrington and Mary Robins, October 15, 1731.

M.   Mary Barron and Joseph Hall, October 13, 1727.

B.   William, son of William and Anne Barton, December 25, 1725.

B.   John, son of John and Christina Bastin, April 11, 1751.

M.   John Bateman and Anne Williams, February 4, 1740/1.

M.   Anne Bateman and John Limit, April 6, 1751.

M.   Thomas Bateman and Winifred Kelly, February 7, 1771.

B.   Reuben, son of James and [blank] Bates, January 24, 1730/1.

M.   Reuben Bates and Sarah Pestridge, December 4, 1757.

B.   William, son of Reuben and Sarah Bates, October 3, 1764.

D.   Thomas Baxter, May 6, 1722.

B.   Anne, daughter of Abraham and Mary Baxter, January 2, 1725/6.

D.   Frances Baxter, January 23, 1725/6.

D.   Abraham Baxter, April 19, 1726.

M.   William Baxter and Mary Rallings, April 1, 1735.

B.   Peggy, daughter of William and Mary Baxter, March 29, 1740.

M.   Anne Baxter of this Parish and Thomas Butler of Washington Parish, September 22, 1742.

B.   John, son of William and Mary Baxter, December 16, 1742.

M.   Mary Baxter and William Jones, July 26, 1744.

B.   Nathaniel, son of William and Mary Baxter, July 24, 1745.

M.   James Baxter and Sarah Sims, October 20, 1764.

M.   James Baxter and Anne Brisse, June 7, 1767.

B. James, son of James and Anne Baxter, October 2, 1769.

M. Mary Beach and John Clift, July 2, 1745.

M. Behethland Beach and James Scribner, November 7, 1773.

D. John Beal, November 26, 1731.

M. John Beattie and Ann Whiting, September 10, 1779.

M. Daniel Beattie and Susannah Rogers, August 2, 1781.

M. John Bedfard and Margaret Golding, August 8, 1729.

M. Christopher Bell and Alice Proudlove, June 4, 1726.

M. Helenor Bell and John McLean, April 14, 1745.

D. John Bengham, a servant of John Mealy, September 4, 1717.

D. Elizabeth Bennett, May 26, 1718.

M. Lucy Bennet and John Rose, October 14, 1731.

M. James Bennet and Elizabeth Hubbud, December 10, 1731.

B. Moses, son of James and Elizabeth Bennett, December 22, 1732.

B. Barbara, daughter of James and Elizabeth Bennet, November 20, 1737.

B. Behethlem, daughter of James and Elizabeth Bennet, February 15, 1739/40.

M. Cossom Bennet and Katherine Bunbury, January 7, 1742/3.

B. Charles Ellis, son of Cossum and Catharine Bennet, August 23, 1752.

M. Jannet Bennet and James Seaton Ryan, April 5, 1763.

M. Behethland Bennet and Hezekiah Kirk, February 10, 1778.

M. William Bennett and Mary Johnston, November 9, 1782.

B. William, son of Charles and Judith Benson, February 16, 1750/1.

M. William Bentley and Jane Bussey, March 14, 1765.

M. Richard Bernard and Elizabeth Storke, August 29, 1729.

B. Richard, son of Richard and Elizabeth Bernard, September 20, 1734.

B. John, son of Richard and Elizabeth Bernard, December 29, 1735.

10

M. William Bernard and Winifred Thornton, November 25, 1750.

B. Grace, daughter of James and Sarah Berry, January 16, 1719/20.

B. Frances, daughter of Joseph and Catherine Berry, November 11, 1721.

B. Joseph, son of Joseph and Catherine Berry, April 27, 1723.

M. James Berry and Grace Powell, May 28, 1723.

B. Benjamin, son of Joseph and Catherine Berry, October 16, 1724.

D. Margaret, daughter of Joseph and Catherine Berry, July 16, 1725.

B. Sarah, daughter of James and Grace Berry, January 15, 1726/7.

B. Margaret, daughter of Joseph and Catherine Berry, June 14, 1726.

M. Enoch Berry and Dulcebella Bunbury, December 12, 1726.

D. Sarah Berry, November 16, 1729.

D. Jane Berry, a child, December 1, 1729.

B. William, son of James and Grace Berry, February 23, 1731/2.

B. Grace, daughter of James and Grace Berry, February 4, 1733/4.

B. Elizabeth, daughter of James and Grace Berry, June 6, 1735.

B. Marmaduke and Virgin Palmer, son and daughter of James and Grace Berry, January 3, 1737/8.

D. James Berry, January 6, 1738/9.

M. Frances Berry and Thomas Golding, January 28, 1738/9.

M. Anne Berry and Samuel Jackson, February 10, 1739/40.

B. Anthony, son of Grace Berry, June 28, 1744.

M. James Berry and Elizabeth Griffin, August 19, 1747.

M. Thomas Berry and Elizabeth Washington, November 19, 1758.

M. Thomas Berry and Sarah Gardiner, October 21, 1784.

M. Mildred Berry and Benjamin Baber, November 10, 1791. [King George County Marriage Register records license issued for this couple May 11, 1790].

M. Enoch Berry and Judith Fowke, November 23, 1791. [King George County
    Marriage Register records license issued for this couple, May 11, 1790.]

M. Rose Berryman of this county and Richard Taliaferro of Essex County,
    June 10, 1726.

M. Behethlem Berryman and Thomas Booth, October 10, 1727.

M. Frances Berryman of Washington Parish and George Foote of this Parish,
    December 3, 1731.

B. John, son of Gilson and Hannah Berryman, June 23, 1742.

M. William Berryman and Rebecca Vowles, September 10, 1743.

B. Behethlehem, daughter of Gilson and Hannah Berryman, March 23, 1743/4.

B. Andrew Gilson, son of Gilson and Hannah Berryman, June 3, 1745.

B. Rose, daughter of Gilson and Rose Berryman, December 28, 1747.

D. Gilson Berryman, Gentleman, April 4, 1749.

M. Sarah Berryman and Cadwallader Dade, August 20, 1752.

M. Behethland Gilson Berryman and John Thornton, December 13, 1761.

B. Gilson Newton, son of John and Martha Berryman, March 28, 1762.

B. Andrew Gilson, son of John and Martha Berryman, April 15, 1764.

B. Hannah, daughter of John and Martha Berryman, April 21, 1766.

B. Sarah Foote, daughter of John and Martha Berryman, October 21, 1768.

B. Millie, daughter of Henry and Mally Besley, April 28, 1747.

M. Margaret Bignell and Michael Kenny, July 29, 1750.

M. Charles Binns and Anne Alexander, October 4, 1759.

M. Justinian Birch and Behethland Dade, June 30, 1777.

M. Peggy Birch and Samuel Johnson, July 28, 1785.

M. Elizabeth Bishop and George Tavener, January 2, 1739/40.

M. Michael Black and Sarah Radford, December 3, 1752.

M. Elizabeth Blackman and Henry Lock, February 6, 1724/5.

M. Theodorick Bland and Sarah Fitzhugh, December 5, 1772.

B. John, son of Theodorick and Sarah Bland, April 1, 1774.

M. [Blank] Blaxton and Mary Dade, October 10, 1777.

M. George Blinkenshop and Jane Butler, February 12, 1739/40.

B. Arthur, son of George and Jane Blinkenship, September 16, 1743.

M. Jane Blinkenship and Nathaniel Price, July 25, 1746.

BOLLING   SEE: BOWLIN : BOWLINE : BOWLING [PAGES 12 & 13]

M. Elizabeth Bolling and John Thornbury, December 14, 1749.

M. Priscilla Bolling and Thomas Phillips, April 13, 1760.

B. William, son of Jesse and Sarah Bolling, June 17, 1772.

M. Elizabeth Bolling and Robert Clift, January 21, 1777.

M. Eleanor Bolton and William Long, May 15, 1749.

B. James, son of Elizabeth Booing, September 8, 1746.

M. Thomas Booth and Behethlem Berryman, October 10, 1727.

D. Behethlem Booth, October 9, 1728.

M. James Boswel and Mary Stuart, April 6, 1744.

B. Mary, daughter of James and Mary Boswell, March 13, 1744/5.

B. James and Thomas, twin sons of James and Mary Boswell, October 24, 1747.

M. Mary Boswell and David Jones, February 18, 1763.

D. Anne, daughter of Daniel and Frances Bourn, August 1, 1718.

D. Frances Bourn, October 23, 1731.

B. Elizabeth, daughter of Daniel and Frances Bowen, January 1, 1721/2.

B. Anne, daughter of Daniel and Frances Bowen, October 2, 1725.

M. James P. Bowie and Mary Anne Bradshaw, September 16, 1788.

M. Elizabeth Bowin and William Skidmore, May 11, 1747.

M. Margaret Bowling and John Frankling, August 18, 1716.

BOWLIN : BOWLINE : BOWLING   SEE: BOLLING : BOWIN : BOWLING

M. Simon Bowline and Anne Newton, December 5, 1722.

B. Elizabeth, daughter of William and Eleanor Bowline, April 28, 1725.

M. Benjamin Bowline and Mary Lathram, July 27, 1725.

M. William Bowline and Sarah Kirk, June 24, 1726.

M. William Bowline and Elizabeth Kidwell, September 7, 1726.

M. Honour Bowling to this Parish and Joseph Dunman of Overwharton Parish, January 4, 1726/7.

B. Kidwell, son of William and Elizabeth Bowling, March 19, 1726/7.

B. Margaret, daughter of William and Eleanor Bowling, August 15, 1727.

M. Simon Bowlin and Elizabeth Newport, June 5, 1728.

M. Betridge Bowlin and Daniel Hammat, November 2, 1728.

M. Thomas Bowling and RachelColclough, November 11, 1729.

B. Anne, daughter of Simon and Martha Boline, February 20, 1730/1.

D. Robert Bowlin, March 11, 1730/1.

B. Anne, daughter of William and Sarah Bowline, June 9, 1731.

B. John Kidwell, son of William and Elizabeth Bowlin, September 13, 1731.

M. Samuel Bowline and Elizabeth Oxford, October 8, 1731.

B. Priscilla, daughter of Thomas and Rachel Bowlin, March 7, 1731/2.

B. Benjamin, son of Benjamin and Mary Bowline, September 18, 1732.

B. William, son of William and Sarah Bowline, May 13, 1733.

B. Sophia, daughter of Simon and Martha Bowling, October 8, 1733.

B. Mary, daughter of Samuel and Mary Bowline, November 4, 1734.

B. John, son of Benjamin and Mary Bowline, November 10, 1734.

B. Elizabeth, daughter of William and Sarah Bowline, June 10, 1735.

D. Simon Bowline, October 25, 1735.

14   SAINT PAUL'S PARISH REGISTER

B.   Robert, son of Simon Bowline, deceased, and Martha, his wife,
     October 26, 1735.

D.   Martha Bowline, October 29, 1735.

B.   Helenor, daughter of Samuel and Elizabeth Bowling, November 30, 1735.

D.   Mary Bowline, December 5, 1735.

B.   Honor, daughter of William and Sarah Bowling, March 8, 1736/7.

M.   Mary Bowling and William Eaton, August 25, 1737.

B.   Elizabeth, daughter of Samuel and Elizabeth Bowling, October 28, 1737.

B.   Stephen, son of Thomas and Rachel Bowling, January 26, 1738/9.

M.   Joseph Bowling and Pelatiah Grafford, July 15, 1738.

B.   Samuel, son of Samuel and Elizabeth Bowline, February 9, 1739/40.

B.   Mary, daughter of William and Sarah Bowling, July 7, 1740.

B.   William, son of Samuel and Elizabeth Bowline, April 20, 1741.

M.   David Bowline and Jane Pilsher, September 10, 1741.

B.   Sarah, daughter of William and Sarah Bowling, May 30, 1742.

B.   Jesse, son of David and Jane Bowline, June 1, 1742.

B.   Margaret, daughter of Samuel and Elizabeth Bowlen, March 26, 1743.

B.   Benjamin, son of Samuel and Elizabeth Bowlin, August 15, 1744.

B.   Anne, daughter of Samuel and Elizabeth Bowline, February 11, 1745/6.

B.   James, son of Samuel and Elizabeth Bowline, February 20, 1747/8.

M.   Behethlem Bowling and John Dey, February 21, 1747/8.

M.   James Bowling and Mary Overhall, February 11, 1750/1.

M.   Rachel Bowling and Joseph Doody, February 13, 1750/1.

M.   Original Bowling and Margaret French, March 18, 1752.

B.   William, son of Rachel Bowling, November 25, 1754.

D.   Captain Samuel Bowman, July 14, 1742.

M. George Boyle and Mary Whiting, June 2, 1778.

M. Thomas Bradley and Sarah Carver, January 8, 1731/2.

B. Elizabeth, daughter of Thomas and Sarah Bradley, May 26, 1732.

M. Mary Anne Bradshaw and James P. Bowie, September 16, 1788.

M. Uriah Bradshaw and Keziah Bragg, February 23, 1791.

M. Margaret Brady and Richard Lee, July 8, 1723.

M. Keziah Bragg and Uriah Bradshaw, February 23, 1791.

D. Amy Brandegan, June 23, 1741.

M. Susanna Brandigen and Samuel Wells, July 8, 1723.

B. Elizabeth, daughter of John and Mary Brannam, February 15, 1735/6.

B. Mary, daughter of John and Mary Brannam, February 5, 1738/9.

D. John Brannam, September 27, 1742.

B. Chloe, daughter of John and Mary Brannam, March 8, 1742/3.

M. Mary Brannam and John Davis, September 8, 1745.

M. Josiah Bransam and Barbara Linsey, August 5, 1742.

D. John Bransom, October 24, 1716.

M. Katherine Bransom and Moses Grigsby of Overwharton Parish, December 1, 1742.

M. Mary Brauner and Anderson White, October 14, 1794.

M. Zachariah Brazier and Elizabeth Buckner, November 12, 1759.

B. William, son of William and Jane Brent of Richland, July 26, 1733.

B. Giles, son of William and Jane Brent of Richland, September 17, 1735.

BRIANT   SEE: BRYAN : BRYANT

B. Henry, son of William and Sarah Briant, April 9, 1756.

B. William, son of William and Mary Briant, March 9, 1760.

M. William Briant and Elizabeth Simpson, June 21, 1779.

M. William Briant and Ursula Burridge, February 27, 1782.

M. Jesse Briant and Anne Norman, January 1, 1790. [King George County Mar-
    riage Register records a license issued for Jesse Bryant and Anne Nor-
    man on December 29, 1789].

M. Mary Bridges of Overwharton Parish and John Devean, August 4, 1764.

M. David Briggs and Jane McDonald, June [blank], 1771.

M. Anne Brisse and James Baxter, June 7, 1767.

M. Sarah Broadburn and Thomas Bunbury, October 15, 1723.

M. Jane Brockenbrough and Thomas Pratt, June 23, 1785.

M. John Brooke and Lucy Thornton, July 2, 1777.

M. Mary Brooke and Elias Rose, March 30, 1778.

B. John, son of Mary Brookes, March 19, 1773.

M. Charity Brown of Hanover Parish and Isaac Suttle, September 24, 1726,
    "per certification from under the Clerk of the Church's hand may appear."

B. Joyce, daughter of Daniel and Elizabeth Brown, March 12, 1727/8.

B. George, son of Daniel Brown, December 23, 1742.

M. William Brown and Elizabeth Butler, August 2, 1744.

B. John, son of William and Elizabeth Brown, February 18, 1744/5.

B. Butler, son of William and Elizabeth Brown, April 10, 1747.

B. William, son of William and Elizabeth Brown, September 23, 1748.

B. Mildred, daughter of William and Elizabeth Brown, December 26, 1757.

B. Lucy, mulatto daughter of Mary Brown, April 1, 1758.

M. James Brown and Sarah Waemark, May 11, 1760.

B. James, son of William and Elizabeth Brown, August 1, 1761.

M. Thomas Brown and Mildred Smith, December 16, 1773.

M. Parthenia Brown and Samuel Franks, January 19, 1786.

M. James Brown and Hannah Mills, January 31, 1786. [King George County Mar-
    riage Register records a license issued for James Browne and Hannah Mills,
    widow, January 27, 1786].

M. William Bruce and Lucinda Pollard, December 20, 1787.

M. William Bruton and Elizabeth Spiler, June 5, 1725.

B. Mary, daughter of William and Elizabeth Bruton, July 4, 1725.

D. Elizabeth Bruton, a child, May 31, 1728.

B. Elizabeth, daughter of William and Elizabeth Bruerton, January 25, 1726/7.

D. Thomas, son of William and Elizabeth Bruton, October 3, 1728.

B. Elizabeth, daughter of William and Elinor Bruton, January 15, 1727/8.

B. Patrick, son of Patrick and Catherine Bruirton, June 2, 1757.

BRYAN : BRYANT   SEE: BRIANT

D. Nathaniel Bryan, March 23, 1732/3.

B. John, son of William and Mary Bryan, May 24, 1735.

B. William, son of William and Mary Bryan, May 6, 1739.

M. John Bryant and Sarah Graham, December 11, 1768.

M. Monica Bryant and John Addison, March 19, 1789.

M. James Buchanan and Elizabeth Limmit, December 7, 1777.

B. Henry, son of Henry and Tabitha Buckeridge, June 12, 1768.

M. Dorothy Buckley and Thomas South, July 10, 1754.

D. Robert Buckner, October 25, 1718.

D. Elizabeth Buckner, November 14, 1725.

D. William Buckner, November 14, 1725.

D. William Buckner, August 3, 1727.

D. Anthony Buckner, March 21, 1733/4.

D. Anthony Buckner, December 1, 1734.

M. Sarah Buckner and Thomas Price, December 31, 1734

D. Major John Buckner, May 6, 1748.

B. Susan, daughter of John and Elizabeth Buckner, September 1, 1751.

B. Parthenia, daughter of Anthony and Amy Buckner, October 14, 1758.

M. Elizabeth Buckner and Zachariah Brazier, November 12, 1759.

M. John Buckner and Elizabeth Washington, December 21, 1760.

M. Thomas Bunbury and Sarah Broadburn, October 15, 1723.

D. William Bunbury, November 14, 1725.

B. John, son of Thomas and Sarah Bunbury, January 2, 1725/6.

M. Dulcebella Bunbury and Enoch Berry, December 12, 1726.

B. William, son of Thomas and Sarah Bunbury, January 26, 1726/7.

B. Mildred, daughter of Thomas and Sarah Bunbury, September 2, 1731.

B. Dolabella, daughter of Thomas and Sarah Bunbury, September 15, 1733.

B. Elizabeth, daughter of Thomas and Sarah Bunbury, April 25, 1736.

D. Frances Bunbury, April 4, 1737.

B. Frances, daughter of Thomas and Sarah Bunbury, September 1, 1738.

M. Jane Bunbury and George Hardin, December 3, 1740.

B. Anne and Jane, twin daughters of Thomas and Sarah Bunbury, November 12, 1741.

M. Katherine Bunbury and Cossom Bennet, January 7, 1742/3.

B. Sarah, daughter of Thomas and Sarah Bunbury, March 9, 1743/4.

M. Dulcebella Bunbury and Withers Conway, April 21, 1752.

M. Thomas Bunbury and Behethland Massey, August 30, 1752.

B. Elizabeth, daughter of Thomas and Behethland Bunbury, January 30, 1756.

M. Mildred Bunbury and William Scott, June 18, 1756.

M. Frances Bunbury and Alexander Scott, February 22, 1758.

M. Anne Bunbury and Richard Fowke, March 16, 1760.

B. Anne, daughter of Thomas and Behethland Bunbury, July 1, 1764.

M. Jane Bunbury and Joseph Sanford, May 8, 1766.

M. Elizabeth Bunbury and Stephen Chandler, December 24, 1774.

M. Frances Bunbury and William Smoot, September 23, 1775.

M. William Bunbury and Elizabeth Short, January 16, 1783.

B. Mary, daughter of Richard and [blank] Burges, November 3, 1736.

M. Lettice Burges and John Engles, February 15, 1736/7.

B. Edward, son of Edward and Margaret Burges, November 27, 1739.

B. Moses, son of Edward and Margaret Burgess, December 2, 1742.

B. Rubin, son of Edward and Margaret Burgess, February 12, 1744/5.

M. Joseph Burgess and Elizabeth Douglas, July 15, 1749.

M. Anne Burgess and Joseph Rogers, October 24, 1749.

M. Margaret Burgess and John French, January 15, 1749/50.

M. Mary Burgess and Nathan Skipweth White, April 15, 1759.

M. Moses Burgess and Elizabeth Price, May 30, 1762.

B. Lunsford, son of Moses and Elizabeth Burgess, September 20, 1762.

B. John Buckner, son of Moses Burgess, April 5, 1764.

M. Edward Burgess and [blank] Price, February 20, 1765.

M. Reuben Burgess and [blank] Stribling, September 1, 1765.

B. Edward, son of Moses and Elizabeth Burgess, April 2, 1767.

B. Mary, daughter of Reuben and Margaret Burgess, July 7, 1767.

B. William, son of Reuben and Margaret Burgess, June 15, 1769.

B. Reuben, son of Reuben and Margaret Burgess, June 14, 1772.

B. William, son of Thomas and Jane Burk, April 2, 1752.

M. William Burke and Susanna Sweney, February 1, 1778.

M. John Burket and Mary Carneby, September 27, 1735.

D. John Burket, October 1, 1736.

B. Helenor, daughter of John and Mary Burket, January 2, 1736/7.

M. Mary Burket and Thomas Norfolk, December 6, 1737.

M. Thomas Burnett and Alice Care of Hanover Parish, June 20, 1746.

B. Mary, daughter of Joseph and Eleanor Burnoin, February 28, 1772.

M. Jethro Burnsplat and Sarah Bagjah, October 21, 1729.

B. Sarah, daughter of Jethro and Sarah Burnsplat, January 16, 1731/2.

B. Helenor, daughter of Jethro and Sarah Burnsplat, March 2, 1735/6.

D. Jethro Burnsplat, November 2, 1737.

M. Sarah Burnsplat and Richard Hill, December 22, 1737.

M. Eleanor Burnsplat and James Kelly, April 15, 1757.

M. Ursula Burridge and William Briant, February 27, 1782.

M. William Burton and Sarah Spicer, December 14, 1725.

B. Lettice, daughter of William and Sarah Burton, August 19, 1726.

B. Mary, daughter of William and Rachel Burton, May 30, 1754.

M. Charity Bush and Peter Cash, November 3, 1729.

M. George Bush and Mary Ancrum, November 14, 1737.

B. William, son of George and Mary Bush, September 8, 1738.

B. Frances, daughter of George and Mary Bush, April 20, 1741.

M. Frances Bush and Joshua Skidmore, August 6, 1751.

M. John Bushel and Elizabeth Mason, June 26, 1748.

B. George, son of Elizabeth Busle, May 20, 1731.

M. Elizabeth Bussle and Andrew Drummond, January 16, 1735/6.

M. Sarah Bussee and Ralph Walker, January 26, 1722/3.

D. Martha Bussey, June 23, 1725.

B. Sarah, daughter of Henry and Elizabeth Bussy, January 22, 1730/1.

B. Anne, daughter of Henry and Elizabeth Bussy, April 19, 1734.

D. Elizabeth Bussy, July 20, 1739.

M.   Henry Bussey and Margaret McCarty, July 11, 1741.

B.   Henry, son of Henry and Margaret Bussy, April 13, 1743.

B.   Cornelius, son of Henry and Margaret Bussy, June 18, 1745.

M.   Mary Bussey and Thomas Mills, January 2, 1748/9.

M.   Anne Bussey and John Matthews, July 21, 1754.

M.   Henry Bussey and Jane Jackson, November 21, 1758.

M.   Jane Bussey and William Bentley, March 14, 1765.

M.   Cornelius Bussey and Mary Carver, October 14, 1770.

M.   Cornelius Bussey and Jane Crawford, June 23, 1776.

Baptized John, son of Thomas and Elizabeth Butler, March 6, 1719/20.

B.   Mary and Elizabeth, daughters of Thomas and Elizabeth Butler, February 12, 1724/5.

D.   Mary and Elizabeth, daughters of Thomas and Elizabeth Butler, February 18, 1724/5.

B.   Elizabeth, daughter of Thomas and Elizabeth Butler, April 15, 1726.

D.   Elizabeth, wife of Thomas Butler, September 22, 1727.

D.   Thomas Butler, July 10, 1728.

M.   Sarah Butler of this Parish and Charles Ashton of Washington Parish, September 22, 1733.

M.   John Butler and Elizabeth Clement, February 19, 1733/4.

M.   Jane Butler and William Knight, December 26, 1734.

D.   Elizabeth Butler, January 19, 1736/7.

B.   Katherine, daughter of James and Sarah Butler, August 24, 1737.

B.   Margaret, daughter of James and [blank] Butler, December 27, 1739.

M.   Jane Butler and George Blinkenshop, February 12, 1739/40.

B.   John, son of James and Sarah Butler, December 27, 1740.

M.   Thomas Butler of Washington Parish and Anne Baxter, September 22, 1742.

B.   Sarah, daughter of James and Sarah Butler, January 17, 1742/3.

M.   Elizabeth Butler and William Brown, August 2, 1744.

B.   Thomas, son of James and Sarah Butler, August 30, 1747.

B.   Joseph, son of Henry and Anne Butrage, July 29, 1759.

B.   Violetta, daughter of John and Elizabeth Buttridge, September 4, 1764.

M.   Henry Butridge and Isabel Hodge, December 30, 1764.

B.   William Matthews, son of John and Elizabeth Buttridge, July 3, 1767.

M.   Violet Buttridge and James Cochley, January 12, 1786.

B.   Anne, daughter of James and Bridget Buzell, August 21, 1738.

B.   George, son of Thomas and Jane Byrne, March 16, 1760.

                                    C

M.   David Cable and Mary Orr, September 7, 1766.

M.   Elizabeth Calb and William Clift, January 16, 1764.

D.   John Calicoe, September 19, 1717.

B.   John, son of John Callico, deceased, and Rebecca, February 19, 1717/8.

D.   John, son of John and Rebecca Callico, May 12, 1720.

M.   Frances Call and Thomas Sweatman, December 16, 1765.

D.   [?]h Campbell, November 27, 1725.

M.   Mary Campbell and Edward Daleny, April 15, 1726.

M.   Katherine Campbell and John Raymond, January 12, 1735/6.

M.   John Campbell and Judith Pilcher of Hanover Parish, August 20, 1746.

B.   William, son of Katherine Campbell, June 12, 1747.

B.   James, son of Christian Campbell, July 17, 1747.

M.   Katherine Campbell and Francis Allan, November 17, 1747.

M.   Archibald Campbell and Rebecca Rallings, January 15, 1753.

M. Alexander Campbell and Lucy Fitzhugh, December 3, 1788.

M. Margaret Cannady and Benjamin Derrick, August 3, 1734.

M. Hugh Cannady and Mildred Hutcheson, November 6, 1735.*

M. Alice Care of Hanover Parish and Thomas Burnett, June 20, 1746.

M. Mary Carneby and John Burket, September 27, 1735.

M. Sarah Carico and Joseph King, May 7, 1731.

M. Thomas Carrico and Jane McCant, October 4, 1744.

B. John, son of Thomas and Jane Carrico, October 7, 1745.

B. Alexander, son of Thomas and Sarah Carrico, February 10, 1746/7.

D. Thomas Carrico, February 5, 1748/9.

M. Mary Carrol and George Harris, July 14, 1750.

M. Rosamond Carroll of Brunswick Parish and Joseph Tucker, February 20, 1733/4.

B. Elizabeth Leftridge, daughter of John and Sarah Carroll, March 8, 1753.

M. Helena Cartee and Richard Turner, September 24, 1725.

M. Anne Carter and John Champe, Junior, April 17, 1762.

M. Richard Carver and Sarah Jones, January 21, 1722/3.

B. John, son of Richard and Sarah Carver, March 19, 1726/7.

M. Thomas Carver and Mary Clift, November 10, 1727.

D. Joseph Carver, December 20, 1727.

M. Sarah Carver and Thomas Bradley, January 8, 1731/2.

B. Joseph, son of Thomas and Mary Carver, November 11, 1732.

D. Richard Carver, December 6, 1732.

M. Frances Carver and John Suthard, June 8, 1733.

B. Jane, daughter of Richard and Sarah Carver, June 23, 1733.

B. Thomas, son of Thomas and Mary Carver, February 20, 1734/5.

---

* See page 78 under Kennedy for a child of this couple.

SAINT PAUL'S PARISH REGISTER

B. William, son of Thomas and Mary Carver, July 5, 1737.

B. William, son of Sarah Carver, November 15, 1737.

B. Sarah, daughter of Thomas and Mary Carver, September 13, 1739.

B. Charles, son of Mary Carver, July 28, 1741.

B. Joseph, son of Thomas and Mary Carver, February 17, 1742/3.

B. Jane, daughter of Thomas and Mary Carver, July 1, 1745.

B. Jane, daughter of Thomas and Mary Carver, January 10, 1747/8.

M. Anne Carver and Burgess Swillivan, February 3, 1747/8.

B. Polly, daughter of Thomas and Mary Carver, October 13, 1750.

B. Frances, daughter of Thomas and Mary Carver, January 24, 1754.

M. Thomas Carver and Rosamond Duncum, August 12, 1755.

M. John Carver and Elizabeth Doggett, August 31, 1757.

B. Thomas, son of William and Sarah Carver, November 2, 1757.

B. Betty, daughter of John and Hannah Carver, February 2, 1760.

B. Molly, daughter of John and Susan Carver, March 26, 1762.

B. Mildred, daughter of William and Mary Carver, May 10, 1762.

B. William, son of William and Sarah Carver, January 4, 1764.

M. Sarah Carver and Daniel Taylour, January 19, 1764.

B. Jane, daughter of Joseph and Elizabeth Carver, December 25, 1765.

M. Jane Carver and Dennis Mehorner, September 8, 1766.

B. William, son of Joseph and Elizabeth Carver, January 9, 1767.

B. Reuben, son of Charles and Mary Carver, October 10, 1767.

M. John Carver and Mary Rose, July 17, 1768.

B. Frances, daughter of Joseph and Elizabeth Carver, January 12, 1769.

B. Elizabeth, daughter of Joseph and Elizabeth Carver, August 12, 1770.

M. Mary Carver and Cornelius Bussey, October 14, 1770.

B. John, son of Charles and Anne Carver, January 27, 1771.

B. Susanna, daughter of Robert and Jane Carver, April 18, 1771.

B. Reuben, son of Joseph and Elizabeth Carver, April 12, 1772.

B. Anne, daughter of John and Mary Carver, May 19, 1773.

B. Joseph, son of Joseph and Elizabeth Carver, January 18, 1773.

B. Thomas, son of Joseph and Elizabeth Carver, May 10, 1774.

B. Reuben, son of Joseph and Elizabeth Carver, November 1, 1777.

B. Henry, son of Joseph and Elizabeth Carver, November 30, 1779.

M. Molly Carver and William Whitmore, January 5, 1781.

B. George, son of Joseph and Elizabeth Carver, September 10, 1782.

M. John Carver and Hannah Clift, April 14, 1784.

M. Dully Carver and Charles Philips, August 19, 1787.

B. Moses, son of William and Anne Cash, March 9, 1717/8.

D. William Cash, April 2, 1720.

D. John Cash, September 25, 1729.

M. Peter Cash and Charity Bush, November 3, 1729.

B. Jane, daughter of Peter and Charity Cash, March 6, 1732/3.

B. John, son of Peter and Charity Cash, September 3, 1735.

B. Frances, daughter of Peter and Charity Cash, November 9, 1738.

B. Katherine, daughter of Peter and Charity Cash, March 9, 1740/1.

B. Charity, daughter of Peter and Charity Cash, November 26, 1743.

M. Stephen Cash and Jemima Grining, May 26, 1747.

M. Margaret Cash and Josias Stone, April 8, 1780.

M. George Catlett and Mary Harrison, November 23, 1758.

M. Rose Cavenoch and Matthew Jones, September 21, 1746.

M. Anne Chambers and Jasper Lloyd, January 7, 1717/8.

M. Anne Chambers and William Garrett, January 28, 1717/8.

M. Elinor Chambers and Patrick Johnson, May 14, 1726.

M. John Champe, Junior, and Anne Carter, April 17, 1762.

M. Thomas Chancellor and Katherine Cooper, March 3, 1723/4.

M. John Chandler and Behethland Rogers, September 17, 1767.

B. Stephen, son of John and Behethland Chandler, July 6, 1768.

B. William Rogers, son of John and Behethland Chandler, September 27, 1772.

M. Stephen Chandler and Elizabeth Bunbury, December 24, 1774.

M. Pearson Chapman and Susanna Alexander, July 31, 1766.

B. Nathaniel, son of Pearson and Susanna Chapman, June 27, 1767.

B. Anne, daughter of Cornelius and Virgin Cheeseman, February 22, 1717/8.

D. Virgin Cheeseman, March 8, 1720/1.

M. Grace Cheesman and Richard Winson, December 31, 1730.
[For WINSON see VINCENT - VINSON]

B. Jacob, son of Anne Cheesman, August 10, 1734.

M. Anne Cheesman and George Johnson, January 9, 1734/5.

D. Cornelius Cheesman, February 9, 1747/8.

M. Kenelm Cheseldine and Frances Taliaferro, August 9, 1768.

M. Richard Chidley and Sarah Fox, December 21, 1722.

B. Rawleigh, son of Rawleigh and Sarah Chinn, January 22, 1758.

CHIVREL : CHIVERAL   SEE: SACHEVEREL : SHIVEREL

M. Joanna Chivrel and William Long, December 30, 1790.

D. Mary Chranig [?], September 30, 1716.

CHRISTY : CHRISTIE : CHRYSTY :

B. William, son of John and Margaret Chrysty, May 27, 1720.

M. Margaret Chrysty and Henry Smith, May 28, 1723.

M. John Christie and Sarah Glover, August 28, 1743.

B. William, son of John and Mary Christie, November 15, 1745.

B. John, son of John and Sarah Christie, January 10, 1747/8.

D. Sarah, wife of John Christie, December 6, 1748.

M. John Christy and Mary Rian, May 4, 1749.

B. Anne, daughter of John and Mary Christy, February 16, 1750/1.

M. John Christie and Elizabeth Griggs, September 12, 1751.

M. Charles Christie and Anne Smith, March 18, 1753.

B. Charity, daughter of John and Elizabeth Christie, August 21, 1754.

B. Peggy, daughter of John and Elizabeth Christie, February 17, 1757.

B. James, son of John and Elizabeth Christie, January 24, 1761.

M. John Christy and Frances Johnson, January 20, 1771.

M. William Christie and Margaret Thompson, June 6, 1775.

M. John Christy and Elizabeth Gray Dudly, October 7, 1785.

M. John Clanton of Hanover Parish and Anne Spicer of this Parish,
    February 17, 1731/2.

B. Benjamin, son of John and Anne Clanton, November 20, 1732.

M. Elizabeth Clark and John Diskine, April 21, 1724.

M. William Clark of Overwharton Parish and Sarah Sanders of Saint Paul's,
    August 5, 1752.

B. William, son of Moses Clark, December 29, 1757.

B. George, son of Moses and Susan Clark, January 26, 1760.

M. Patrick Clarke and Tabitha Kelly, August 13, 1764.

M. Charles Clarke and Phebe Derrick, December 14, 1785.

M. Mary Clark and James Talmash, May 17, 1792.

D. Grace Clement, August 6, 1727.

M. Edward Clement and Elizabeth Fruyn, October 25, 1728.

D. Edward Clement, June 20, 1733.

M. Elizabeth Clement and John Butler, February 19, 1733/4.

B. Benjamin and Sarah, son and daughter of John and Hannah Clift, August 5, 1717.

D. Hannah Clift, November 27, 1725.

M. Mary Clift and Thomas Carver, November 10, 1727.

M. William Clift and Mary Hill, January 19, 1730/1.

M. John Clift and Margaret Johns, March 2, 1738/9.

M. Sarah Clift and John Linsey, January 3, 1739/40.

B. William, son of John and Mary Clift, March 28, 1740.

M. Benjamin Clift and Margaret Sebastian, May 6, 1740.

B. John, son of John and Margaret Clift, May 1, 1742.

B. William, son of John and Margaret Clift, October 28, 1742.

M. Joseph Clift and Joyce Barret, June 22, 1743.

B. Thomas, son of Joseph and Joyce Clift, September 22, 1744.

M. John Clift and Mary Beach, July 2, 1745.

B. Nanny, daughter of Benjamin and Margaret Clift, May 6, 1746.

B. Robert, son of John and Mary Clift, September 8, 1746.

B. Hannah, daughter of Joseph and Joyce Clift, May 5, 1748.

B. Benjamin, son of John and Mary Clift, January 17, 1748/9.

B. Joseph, son of Robert and Jane Clift, December 5, 1750.

B. Henry, son of John and Mary Clift, January 4, 1750/1.

B. Catherine, daughter of Robert and Jane Clift, February 26, 1753.

B. Polly, daughter of John and Mary Clift, September 28, 1753.

B. Billy, son of Benjamin and Margaret Clift, January 22, 1754.

B. Anne, daughter of Robert and Jane Clift, August 6, 1755.

B. Sarah, daughter of John Clift, November 5, 1756.

B. Jane, daughter of Robert and Jane Clift, February 3, 1758.

B. Hannah, daughter of John and Mary Clift, February 26, 1760.

B. Molly, daughter of Robert and Jane Clift, May 23, 1760.

B. Robert, son of Robert and Jane Clift, September 21, 1762.

M. William Clift and Elizabeth Calb, January 16, 1764.

B. Reuben, son of John and Mary Clift, July 6, 1764.

B. John, son of Robert and Jane Clift, November 12, 1764.

M. Benjamin Clift and Frances Peak, February 16, 1772.

M. Benjamin Clift and Sarah Rogers, December 6, 1772.

M. Robert Clift and Elizabeth Bolling, January 21, 1777.

M. John Clift and Jemima Arnold, December 26, 1777.

M. John Clift and Anne Rodgers, September 29, 1779.

M. Caty Clift and Hosea Rogers, January 22, 1783.

M. Hannah Clift and John Carver, April 14, 1784.

M. Dully Clift and John Scott, February 15, 1787.

M. Robert Clift and Peggy Munda, January 6, 1793. [King George County Marriage Register records a license issued to Robert Clift and Peggy Minor, January 5, 1793].

M. Anne Clifton and William Scott, February 23, 1727/8.

M. Burdet Clifton and Frances Hill, July 15, 1733.

B. Thomas, son of Burdet and Frances Clifton, April 20, 1734.

B. Burdet and Baldwin, twin sons of Burdet and Frances Clifton, February 3, 1735/6.

B. Anne, daughter of Burdet and Frances Clifton, August 24, 1737.

B. Sarah, daughter of Burdet and Frances Clifton, April 10, 1740.

B. Jane and Elizabeth, twin daughters of Burdet and Frances Clifton, May 14, 1743.

M. Burdit Clifton and Grace Seaton, May 18, 1745.

B. Henry, son of Burdet and Grace Clifton, March 17, 1745/6.

B. Charles, son of Burdet and Grace Clifton, December 12, 1747.

B. John, son of Thomas and Anne Clifton, February 7, 1758.

M. Ann Clifton and Price Stuart, October 17, 1781.

M. [Blank] Coad and Elizabeth Massey, December [blank], 1766.

M. James Cochley and Violet Buttridge, January 12, 1786.

    COGGANS : COGGENS : COGGINS : AND SIMILIAR SPELLINGS

D. [Torn] Coggins, April 29, 1717.

M. Rose Cogins and William Cook, July 22, 1717.

M. John Coggen and Sophia Gotley, February 22, 1736/7.

B. Anna, daughter of John and Sophia Coggan, March 30, 1737.

B. Amos, son of John and Sophia Coggen, March 23, 1738/9.

B. Betty, daughter of John and Sophia Coggan, November 13, 1740.

M. William Coheley and Mildred Sullivan, February 4, 1781.

B. William and Alexander, sons of Benjamin and Rachel Colclough, July 2,
    1717.

B. Sarah, daughter of Benjamin and Rachel Colclough, March 17, 1719/20.

M. Hester Colclough and Joel Stribling, September 25, 1723.

M. Rachel Colclough and Thomas Bowling, November 11, 1729.

D. Alexander Colclough, November 10, 1739.

M. Jane Colclough of this Parish and Benjamin Newton of Hamilton Parish,
    October 22, 1740.

M. William Colclough and Mary Rogers, December 30, 1741.

B. John, son of William and Mary Colclough, September 14, 1743.

B. Margaret, daughter of William and Mary Colclough, February 4, 1744/5.

B. Elizabeth, daughter of William and Mary Colclough, October 11, 1747.

D.   Rachel Colclough, December 25, 1748.

B.   Samuel Cole, a Mustee, May 6, 1726.

B.   Elizabeth, daughter of Mary Colins, November 25, 1736.

M.   Mary Collins and William Stevenson, September 24, 1761.

B.   Mary, daughter of John and Elizabeth Collins, March 22, 1762.

B.   James, son of Anne Colsworth, September 30, 1747.

B.   Mason, son of Daniel Colven, February 26, 1764 (Overwharton).

M.   Margaret Colvin and William Ankrum, December 24, 1734.

M.   John Conah and Helen Fog, June 22, 1724.

M.   John Conah and Elinor Ormond, June 13, 1725.

D.   Elinor Conner, a servant woman belonging to Samuel Todd, September 3, 1718.

B.   Withers, son of Christopher and Sarah Conway, August 20, 1717.

M.   Elizabeth Conway and John Alsop, December 30, 1739.

M.   Withers Conway and Dulcebella Bunbury, April 21, 1752.

B.   Miles Withers, son of Withers and Dulicibella Conway, March 2, 1753.

B.   John Withers, son of Withers and Dulcibella Conway, September 12, 1757.

B.   Anne, daughter of Withers and Dulcibella Conway, April 13, 1764.

M.   William Cook and Rose Cogins, July 22, 1717.

M.   Rose Cook and William Hawkins, August 16, 1723.

M.   Joseph Cook and Mary Trenar, December 26, 1723.

B.   Elizabeth, daughter of William and Elizabeth Cooper, May 3, 1718.

M.   Katherine Cooper and Thomas Chancellor, March 3, 1723/4.

B.   Jane, daughter of Mary Cooper, December 5, 1737.

B.   James, son of Elizabeth Cooper, December 8, 1740.

M.   Elizabeth Cooper and Robert Suddath, October 2, 1750.

M. James Cope and Elizabeth Miflin of Hanover Parish, December 17, 1746.

M. Anne Coplee of this Parish and John Tracy of Washington Parish, August 7, 1740.

M. Katherine Copley and John Wilkison, August 14, 1743.

M. Margaret Corbin and William Griffin, April 6, 1725.

M. John Corbin and Lettice Lee, September 1, 1737.

M. Rosamond Corbin of this Parish and John Spinks of Brunswick Parish, November 6, 1741.

M. Mary Cotes and Samuel Wilkinson, December 9, 1734.

M. Anne Coventry and Joseph Sebastian, September 8, 1751.

B. Matthew, son of Matthew and Mary Cox, September 19, 1745.

M. Richard Cox and Anne Crisman, September 2, 1750.

    CRAFFORD : CRAFFORT : GRAFFORD : GRAFFORT

B. Pelatiah, daughter of Philip and Pelatya Crafford, May 4, 1718.

B. Philip, son of Philip and Pelatya Grafford, [torn], 1723.

D. Palater Graffort, June 18, 1725.

M. Philip Crafford and Mary Simmons, November 27, 1730.

B. Peter, son of Philip and Mary Grafford, September 15, 1731.

B. William, son of Philip and Mary Crafford, November 2, 1734.

D. John Crafford, December 20, 1736.

M. Pelatiah Grafford and Joseph Bowling, July 15, 1738.

B. Mary, daughter of Mary Crafford, March 4, 1738/9.

M. Peter Crafford and Jane Gladsteans, August 7, 1755.

M. William Crank and Sabry Jones, February 8, 1778.

B. Onner, daughter of Jeremy and Onner Crannedge, February 2, 1717/8.

D. Honour Crannige, June 26, 1735.

M. Samuel Crannidge and Elizabeth Dey, May 6, 1741.

B. Mary, daughter of Samuel and Elizabeth Crannidge, September 20, 1741.

B. Jane, daughter of Samuel and Elizabeth Crannidge, October 8, 1743.

B. Samuel, son of Samuel and Elizabeth Crannidge, March 12, 1744/5.

M. Jane Crawford and Cornelius Bussey, June 23, 1776.

    CRISMAN : CRISMAND : CRISMUND : CHRISMUND

M. Anne Crisman and Richard Cox, September 2, 1750.

M. Joseph Crismand and Elizabeth Purtle, February 16, 1752.

M. Oswald Chrismund and Jane Rose, June 27, 1757.

B. Oswald, son of Oswald and Jane Crismund, September 2, 1760.

B. Charles, son of Oswald and Jane Crismund, August 8, 1764.

B. John, son of Oswald and Jane Crismund, March 27, 1766.

M. William Chrismund and Anne Tregar, April 28, 1779.

M. Robert Crook and Mary Gosselen, April 15, 1745.

Baptized John, son of Dennis and Margaret Cruyers, June 6, 1725.

B. Thomas, son of Adam and Anna Barbara Crump, February 17, 1734/5.

B. John, son of Adam and Anna Barbara Crump, September 28, 1736.

D. Anna Barbara Crump, December 12, 1737.

M. William Crysell and Frances Rose, November 17, 1782.

M. John Culham and Lettice Suthard, February 17, 1775.

M. James Cullings and Sarah Hutton, February 14, 1755.

M. Peter Culvy and Sarah Sweney, March 28, 1758.

M. Morice Cunningham and Anne Poplar, April 2, 1738.

B. Phebe, daughter of Morrice and Anne Cunningham, April 6, 1739.

M. James Cunningham and Behethland Overhall, June 21, 1757.

M. Elizabeth Cupper and Jasper Floid, December 4, 1723.

M. John Curley and Mary Maddox, May 9, 1767.

B. David, son of John and Mary Curley, February 16, 1773.

M. John Curry and Jane Stribling, September 20, 1758.

M. Jane Curry and William Peck, August 3, 1766.

M. John Curry and Anne Rogers, December 25, 1783.

                                    D

B. Baldwin, son of Townshend and Elizabeth Dade, October 13, 1716.

D. Jane, daughter of Francis and Jane Dade, May 14, 1718.

D. Francis Dade, Junior, December 3, 1725.

D. Behethlem Dade, January 19, 1725/6.

M. Henry Dade and Elizabeth Massey, July 7, 1726.

B. Frances, daughter of Townshend and Elizabeth Dade, August 30, 1726.

B. Mary, daughter of Henry and Elizabeth Dade, June 11, 1727.

B. Horatio, son of Townshend and Elizabeth Dade, [torn; circa 1728-1729].

B. Robert, son of Henry and Elizabeth Dade, May 14, 1731.

B. Frances Townshend, daughter of Townshend and Elizabeth Dade, October 7,
    1732.

B. Frances, daughter of Henry Dade, March 12, 1733/4.

D. Elizabeth, wife of Henry Dade, March 18, 1733/4.

B. Elizabeth, daughter of Townshend and Elizabeth Dade, October 20, 1734.

M. Townshend Dade, Junior, and Parthenia Massey, May 6, 1736.

M. Baldwin Dade and Sarah Alexander, August 7, 1736.

B. Cadwallader, son of Townshend and Elizabeth Dade, December 26, 1736,
    and died soon after.

D. Elizabeth, wife of Townshend Dade, December 30, 1736.

B. Anne Fowke, daughter of Townshend and Parthenia Dade, December 13, 1737.

B. Francis, son of Baldwin and Sarah Dade, December 29, 1737.

D. Sarah, wife of Baldwin Dade, October 30, 1739.

M. Robert Dade and Elizabeth Harrison, January 4, 1742/3.

M. Langhorn Dade and Mildred Washington, February 14, 1742/3.

B. Townshend, son of Langhorn and Mildred Dade, December 25, 1743.

D. Sarah, wife of Cadwallader Dade, February 13, 1743/4.

D. Jane, wife of Francis Dade, May 23, 1744.

B. Behethlehem Alexander, daughter of Robert and Elizabeth Dade, December 23, 1744.

M. Townshend Dade and Rose Grigsby, December 12, 1745.

B. Cadwallader, son of Langhorn and Mildred Dade, January 1, 1745/6.

M. Mary Dade and Howson Hooe, Junior, September 26, 1746.

B. Sarah, daughter of Baldwin and Linny Dade, January 20, 1746/7.

B. Jane, daughter of Langhorn and Mildred Dade, April 2, 1748.

D. Jane, daughter of Langhorn and Mildred Dade, September 28, 1748.

M. Horatio Dade and Frances Richards, October 5, 1749.

M. Elizabeth Dade and Robert Yates, February 17, 1750/1.

M. Elizabeth Dade and Lawrence Washington, July 31, 1751.

M. Cadwallader Dade and Sarah Berryman, August 20, 1752.

M. Horatio Dade and Mary Massey, January 14, 1753.

B. Franky, daughter of Horatio and Mary Dade, October 10, 1753.

M. Frances Dade and Charles Stuart, August 6, 1754.

M. Mildred Dade and Walter Williamson, March 1, 1755.

M. Frances Dade and Francis Peyton, April 24, 1755.

B. Horatio, son of Horatio and Mary Dade, August 25, 1757.

B. Hannah Gibbons, daughter of Horatio and Mary Dade, July 1, 1759.

B. Baldwin, son of Baldwin and Verlinda Dade, February 14, 1760.

B.   Townshend, son of Cadwallader and Sarah Dade, October 28, 1760.

M.   Sarah Dade and Nehemiah Rodham Mason, February 12, 1762.

B.   Elizabeth, daughter of Baldwin and Verlinda Dade, June 13, 1764.

B.   Townshend, son of Horatio and Mary Dade, June 3, 1766.

M.   Townshend Dade and Jane Stuart, December 11, 1769.

M.   Anne Dade and Buckner Stith, February 26, 1772.

M.   Sarah Dade and Lawrence Taliaferro, February 3, 1774.

M.   Frances Dade and James Gwatkin, March 25, 1774.

B.   Townshend Stuart, son of Townshend and Jane Dade, August 4, 1774.

D.   Jane, wife of Townshend Dade and daughter of the Reverend William
     Stuart and Sarah, his wife, August 10, 1774.

M.   Jane Dade and Robert Yates, April 11, 1777.

M.   Behethland Dade and Justinian Birch, June 30, 1777.

M.   Mary Dade and [blank] Blaxton, October 10, 1777.

M.   Hannah Gibbons Dade and Lawrence Ashton, February [blank], 1779.

M.   Elizabeth Dade and Townshend Dade, August 5, 1782.

M.   Sally Dade and James Park, March 4, 1796.

M.   John Dagg and Sarah Overhall, November 14, 1729.

B.   Mary, daughter of John and Sarah Dagg, January 3, 1730/1.

B.   John, son of John and Sarah Dagg, January 20, 1732/3.

B.   William, son of John and Sarah Dagg, February 20, 1734/5.

B.   Sarah, daughter of John and Sarah Dagg, May 5, 1737.

B.   Willibe, son of Margaret Dakings, March 20, 1739/40.

M.   Elizabeth Dalbin and William Jameson, December 30, 1725.

D.   Elizabeth Dalby, January 23, 1727/8.

M.   Edward Daleny and Mary Campbell, April 15, 1726.

M.   Richard Dane and Elizabeth Kelly, June 30, 1746.

M. Anne Darbin and Alexander Murphy, April 8, 1724.

M. Mary Dart and John Fullager, January 26, 1761.

   DAVIS : DAVIES

M. Rachel Davies and William Embrey, October 6, 1743.

B. Martha, daughter of Peter and Martha Davis, July 29, 1735.

D. Peter Davis, July 23, 1736.

M. Martha Davies and John Stone, May 16, 1739.

M. John Davis and Mary Brannam, September 8, 1745.

B. Anne, daughter of William and Isabel Davis, October 23, 1745.

M. Rebecca Davis and Eli Stone, December 4, 1746.

B. James, son of William and Isabella Davis, April 17, 1747.

B. Isaac, son of John and Mary Davies, June 4, 1747.

M. John Davis and Sarah Haukins, August 7, 1750.

B. William, son of William and Isabel Davis, June 14, 1751.

B. Elizabeth, daughter of John and Sarah Davis, January 29, 1752.

M. William Davis and Sarah Franklin, May 13, 1752.

M. Martha Davis and William Mannan, August 13, 1752.

B. Lucy, daughter of William and Ruth Davis, August 26, 1757.

B. Abraham, son of Betty Davis, March 3, 1758.

M. Henry Davis and Margaret Mills, November 5, 1758.

   DAY : DEY

B. Sarah, daughter of Thomas and Elizabeth Day, August 22, 1726.

M. Elizabeth Day of Strother's Parish and Anthony Mislin, May 5, 1735.

M. Sarah Day and William Rose, June 6, 1737.

B. Francis, son of Elizabeth Day, September 16, 1739.

M. Elizabeth Dey and Samuel Crannidge, May 6, 1741.

M. Sarah Day of Hanover Parish and Charles Regg, July 17, 1746.

M. John Dey and Behethlem Bowling, February 21, 1747/8.

M. John Day and Margaret Smith, May 15, 1758.

M. John Deacon and Mary Sacheveral, May 15, 1785.

M. Ambrose Deakins and Victory Simms, May 24, 1789.

D. Mary, daughter of Robert and Elizabeth Dearing, September 7, 1717.

B. Jane, daughter of John and Mary Debell, May 3, 1735.

M. Mary Magdelene Declore and John Whitcraft, September 25, 1716.

DELANDER : DELAUNDER

D. Abram Delaunder, June 29, 1716.

M. Mary Delaunder and Patrick Morrow, October 6, 1716.

M. Helenor Delander and Jacob Johnson, December 10, 1728.

M. Mary Delander and Samuel Jackson, February 21, 1736/7.

D. Abraham Delander, October 25, 1740.

B. Winifred, daughter of Lydia Delisse, December 7, 1768.

M. John Demsoe and Jane Knight, July 6, 1737.

B. Anne, daughter of John and Jane Demse, June 9, 1738.

B. Elliot, son of John and Jane Demse, August 5, 1740

M. Thomas Dennet and Mary Horsey, June 18, 1758.

B. Margaret, daughter of Henry and Anne Dennis, December 3, 1725.

D. Henry Dennis, November 14, 1725.

M. Anne Dennis and Michael Price, August 24, 1727.

M. William Dere and Sarah Head, September 16, 1773.

D. Catherine, daughter of Mathew Derrick, October 8, 1716.

B. Thomas, son of Maddox and Frances Derrick, March 3, 1717/8.

B. Sarah, daughter of Maddox and Frances Derrick, August [?], 1722.

M. Clary Derrick and Robert Mannard, May 27, 1723.

D. Frances, wife of Matthew Derrick, January 12, 1725/6.

M. Edward Derrick and Jemima Powel, January 2, 1728/9.

M. Benjamin Derrick and Mary Neal, September 30, 1729.

B. Elizabeth, daughter of Edward and Jemima Derrick, January 3, 1731/2.

M. Anne Derrick and Benoni Strutton, December 24, 1733.

B. John, son of Edward and Jemima Derrick, February 2, 1733/4.

B. Anne, daughter of Jane Derrick, July 20, 1734.

M. Benjamin Derrick and Margaret Cannaday, August 3, 1734.

D. Margaret Derrick, December 2, 1734.

B. Thomas, son of Edward and Jemima Derrick, April 2, 1736.

M. Benjamin Derrick and Katherine Powel, July 29, 1737.

B. Mary, daughter of Edward and Katherine Derrick, September 30, 1737.

B. Jamima, daughter of Edward and Jemima Derrick, March 6, 1738/9.

B. Behethlem, daughter of Benjamin and Katherine Derrick, September 6, 1739.

D. Edward Derrick, April 27, 1740.

B. Benjamin, son of Benjamin and Katherine Derrick, June 3, 1741.

M. Jemima Derrick and John Thomas, August 10, 1741.

M. Sarah Derrick and John Turner, October 2, 1741.

B. Thomas, son of Benjamin and Katherine Derrick, August 7, 1743.

B. Maddox, son of Benjamin and Katherine Derrick, September 28, 1745.

D. Maddox Derrick, January 8, 1745/6.

B. Edward, son of Benjamin and Katherine Derrick, November 7, 1748.

B. John, son of Benjamin and Katherine Derrick, September 18, 1750.

M. Elizabeth Derrick and William Stribling, January 7, 1753.

B. Sarah, daughter of Benjamin and Catharine Derrick, March 8, 1753.

M. Benjamin Derrick and Martha Whiting, January 31, 1763.

B. Mary, daughter of Benjamin and Martha Derrick, January 27, 1766.

M. Martha Derrick and John Turner, September 2, 1769.

M. Phebe Derrick and Charles Clarke, December 14, 1785.

M. John Devean and Mary Bridges of Overwharton Parish, August 4, 1764.

M. Margaret Dew of Hanover Parish and William Kelley, April 24, 1732.

    DEY   SEE: DAY

M. William Dick and Sarah Lloyd, July 25, 1732.

M. Susanna Dickerson and James Barber, September 5, 1779.

M. Jane Dinsford and Duncan Simson, December 27, 1732.

M. Anne Dishman of Washington Parish and Thomas Grigsby of Overwharton
    Parish, November 25, 1729, by license.

M. John Diskine and Elizabeth Clark, April 21, 1724.

B. William, son of Peter and Elizabeth Dixon, January 12, 1717/8.

M. Richard Dixon and Anne Ramsay, April 13, 1775.

M. Molly Dodd and John Russell, December 18, 1791.

M. Bushrod Dogged of Brunswick Parish and Anne Stribling of this Parish,
    October 6, 1737.

M. Elizabeth Dogget and John Carver, August 31, 1757.

M. William Doick and Esther Jordan, December 20, 1762.

M. Anne Donahoo and John Hammet, August 15, 1757.

B. Alexander, son of Alexander and Sarah Doniphan, August 13, 1721.

M. Sarah Doniphan and William Hansford, February 12, 1725/6, by license.

M. Joseph Doody and Rachel Bowling, February 13, 1750/1.

B. Francis, son of Joseph and Rachel Doody, June 10, 1751.

B. Henry, son of Thomas and Margaret Douglas, March 25, 1738.

B. Mary, daughter of Thomas and Margaret Douglas, April 10, 1740.

M. Alexander Douglas and Keziah Riggins, May 21, 1749.

M. Elizabeth Douglas and Joseph Burgess, July 15, 1749.

B. William, son of Alexander and Keziah Douglas, July 16, 1750.

M. Alexander Douglas and Sarah Martin, September 8, 1751.

B. Thomas, son of Alexander and Sarah Douglas, August 9, 1752.

B. John, son of Alexander and Keziah Douglas, October 14, 1752.

B. John, son of Alexander and Keziah Douglas, March 15, 1756.

B. Anne, daughter of Alexander and Keziah Douglas, October 24, 1757.

B. Jane, daughter of Alexander and Keziah Douglas, January 17, 1761.

M. John Douling and Lettice Speerman of Washington Parish, May 1, 1746.

M. Grace Dounton and James Seaton, March 11, 1730/1.

B. Anne, daughter of Mildred Dounton, March 3, 1759.

M. Frances Dounton and John Johnston, July 30, 1778.

M. Andrew Drummond and Elizabeth Bussle, January 16, 1735/6.

B. Margaret, daughter of Andrew and Elizabeth Drummond, June 6, 1737.

B. James, son of Andrew and Elizabeth Drummond, March 12, 1738/9.

M. Leila Drummond and Henry Duval Maugeur, April 30, 1758.

M. John Duckett and Elizabeth Skidmore, August 6, 1751.

B. James, son of Elizabeth Ducksworth, February 22, 1730/1.

M. Elizabeth Gray Dudly and John Christy, October 7, 1785.

B. James, son of James and Mary Duff, April 5, 1762.

B. Judith, daughter of Susanna Duke, December 12, 1742.

M. Judith Duke and Jeremiah Payne, May 25, 1760.

D. Peter Dukson, Mate of the Ship Exchange, September 2, 1738.

M. Mildred Duling and William Spilman, December 22, 1787.

M. Verlinda Dunahoo and John Taylor, December 13, 1776.

M. John Dunbar and Elizabeth Elliot, September 26, 1752.

B. Susan, daughter of John and Elizabeth Dunbar, March 23, 1755.

M. Mary Duncan and John Smith, November 15, 1722.

M. Sicily Duncan and Patrick Johnson, November 17, 1724.

M. John Duncan and Lettice Woaker, September 27, 1735.

B. Thomas, son of John and Lettice Duncum, July 5, 1736.

D. Thomas Duncan, March 17, 1742/3.

DUNCOMB : DUNCUM   SEE: DUNCAN

B. Benjamin, son of Thomas and Mary Duncomb, November 10, 1721.

B. Rose, daughter of Thomas and Sarah Duncomb, May 16, 1726.

M. Joyce Duncum and Richard Barret, September 21, 1729.

M. Elizabeth Duncum and Thomas Norman, February 21, 1736/7.

D. John, son of Thomas Duncum, September 1, 1740.

D. Mary, wife of Thomas Duncomb, December 8, 1741.

M. Mildred Duncomb and William Williams, December 8, 1743.

B. John, son of Benjamin Duncomb by Sarah Pestridge, December 28, 1748.

M. Rosamond Duncum and Thomas Carver, August 12, 1755.

M. Thomas Duncum and Sarah Whiting, June 2, 1758.

M. Elinor Dunfee and Edward Oxives, November 27, 1724.

D. John Dunkirk, April 2, 1726.

B. James, son of Mary Dunlop, August 6, 1735.

B. Charlotte, daughter of Lydia Dunlop, April 18, 1773.

M. Joseph Dunman of Overwharton Parish and Honour Bowling of this Parish, January 4, 1726/7.

D. Mary Dunn, December 23, 1734.

B. Mealy, son of Samuel and Mary Durham, March 20, 1716/7.

B. Sarah, daughter of Samuel and Mary Durham, October 13, 1717.

B. Edward, son of Samuel and Mary Durham, September 2, 1725.

M. Helen Durham and Robert Raddish, November 10, 1727.

B. Frances, daughter of Samuel and Mary Durham, February 24, 1727/8.

D. Samuel Durham, November 23, 1735.

B. Jane, daughter of William and Margaret Durham, October 2, 1739.

M. Matthew Dyal and Jane Wood, January 23, 1738/9.

B. Reuben, son of Avery Dye, March 27, 1749.

B. Mary, daughter of William and Elizabeth Dye, December 5, 1753.

M. George Dye and Rebecca Dye, March 10, 1790.

                                    E

B. Sarah, daughter of Robert and Jane Eangles, November 4, 1737.

B. Sarah, daughter of Jonathan and Jane Eaton, April 28, 1726.

M. Frances Eaton and Thomas Fleeming, April 10, 1735.

B. William, son of Elizabeth Eaton, May 20, 1735.

M. William Eaton and Mary Bowling, August 25, 1737.

M. John Eddeson and Anne Stratton, July 12, 1751.

B. Katherine, daughter of Sarah Edgar, March 7, 1745/6.

M. Sarah Edrington of Sittingbourne Parish and Thomas Ammon, January 24, 1733/4.

M. Nancy Edrington and William Ashmore, January 14, 1781.

B. Haden, son of William and Mary Edwards of Washington Parish, March 16, 1715/6 and baptized April 15, 1716.

M. Mary Edwards and [torn], May 1, 1717.

M. Elizabeth Edwards and Patrick Ryan, May 6, 1723.

M. Hannah Edwards and Michael Summers, May 12, 1724.

M. Mary Edwards and Charles Wells, December 10, 1733.

B. Jemima, daughter of Mary Edwards, March 4, 1736/7.

M. Mary Edwards and John Philips, February 27, 1737/8.

M. Gustavus Elgin and Anne Sutherland, March 26, 1793.

M. Jean Elkin and Bartholomew Redman, June 24, 1727.

M. Margaret Elkins and Jarret Stevens, June 21, 1727.

M. Priscilla Elkins and Benjamin Sebastian, February 16, 1729/30.

D. Anne Eliot, June 22, 1725.

M. Anne Elliot and Nicholas Sebastian, October 29, 1726.

M. George Elliot and Mary Adams, April 26, 1728.

B. Thomas, son of George and Mary Elliot, February 28, 1731/2.

D. Charles Elliot, October 23, 1734.

B. Elizabeth, daughter of George and Mary Elliot, October 10, 1734.

B. Katherine, daughter of George and Mary Elliot, December 10, 1736.

D. Mary Elliot, July 24, 1738.

B. Jane, daughter of George and Mary Elliot, December 20, 1738.

B. Joseph, son of George and Mary Elliot, May 22, 1740.

B. George, son of George and Mary Elliot, March 31, 1742.

B. Anne, daughter of George and Mary Elliot, July 17, 1743.

B. William Adams, son of George and Mary Elliot, November 17, 1744.

D. Doctor Robert Elliot, March 20, 1743/4.

B. Charles, son of George and Mary Elliot, October 6, 1746.

M. Mary Elliot and Thomas Skinner, December 26, 1749.

M. Sarah Elliot and Absolom Suddath, October 2, 1750.

M. Elizabeth Elliot and John Dunbar, September 26, 1752.

M. William Elliot and Sarah Sharpe, December 17, 1752.

M. Mary Ellis and John Overhall, October 8, 1722.

D. Sarah Ellis, January 19, 1725/6.

M. Mary Ellis and John Harrod, August 4, 1728.

EMBRY : EMBRIE   SEE: AMBRY : AMBRIE

B. Elizabeth, daughter of William and Anne Embrie, November 22, 1726.

M. William Embry and Rachel Davies, October 6, 1743.

B. Eli, son of William and Rachel Embry, April 8, 1745.

D. John Embry, October 5, 1746.

B. John, son of William and Rachel Embry, July 26, 1748.

M. Frances Embry and Thomas Elliot Sebastian, June 4, 1751.

M. Elizabeth Embry and James Sims, October 14, 1762.

M. Thomas Emmerson and Anne McKey, April 17, 1743.

ENGLES : ENGLIS : INGLES

M. John Engles and Lettice Burges, February 15, 1736/7.

B. Sarah, daughter of John and Lettice Engles, February 1, 1737/8.

B. Lettice, daughter of John and Lettice Engles, August 8, 1739.

B. John, son of John and Lettice Engles, February 1, 1740/1.

B. Margaret, daughter of John and Lettice Engles, June 24, 1743.

B. Anne, daughter of John and Lettice Engles, October 12, 1745.

B. Sarah, daughter of John and Lettice Ingles, July 24, 1748.

B. Letty, daughter of John and Lettice Englis, February 23, 1750/1.

B. John, son of John and Lettice Engles, June 3, 1752.

B. Lettice, daughter of J. Englis, October 20, 1753.

B. Robert, son of John and Lettice Engles, July 25, 1756.

B. William, son of John and Letitia Englis, May 7, 1759.

D. Robert English, December 3, 1732.

D. Thomas Ennis, a servant boy belonging to Dennis Conner, September 16, 1721.

M. Elizabeth Evans of this Parish and Patrick Matthews of Nanjemey Parish, August 17, 1725.

B. Virgin, a free mulatto daughter of Elizabeth Evans, September 3, 1726.

B. Katharine, a free mulatto daughter of Elizabeth Evans, April 12, 1730.

B. Jemima, a free mulatto daughter of Elizabeth Evans, May 2, 1735.

B. Lawrence, a free mulatto son of Elizabeth Evans, November 18, 1736.

B. Bathsheba, a free mulatto daughter of Elizabeth Evans, September 29, 1738.

B. Evans, a free mulatto son of Elizabeth Evans, August 6, 1740.

B. Bethia, a free mulatto daughter of Elizabeth Evans, May 25, 1742.

B. Lettis, a free mulatto daughter of Elizabeth Evans, January 25, 1744.

B. Barbara, a free mulatto daughter of Elizabeth Evans, December 19, 1745.

[Of the above nine children of Elizabeth Evans the first two are not recorded in the Register proper but the last seven are. However, all nine are recorded in the back of the Register in the handwriting of the Reverend David Stuart who states "this is a true account of the ages of Elizabeth Evans's children"].

M. Samuel Evans and Jane Riggin, June 29, 1746.

B. John, son of Samuel and Jane Evans, December 18, 1746.

M. Thomas Evans and Anne Lucas, February 4, 1753.

B. Sarah, daughter of Thomas and Anne Evans, January 17, 1754.

M. Jane Evans and [blank] Friar, December 1, 1769.

M. Bethia Evans and Thomas Mehorner, March 30, 1786.

B. Denis, son of Martin and Mary Farrel, September 27, 1742.

B. William, son of Martin and Mary Farrel, April 27, 1745.

M. Margaret Fauman and William Ward, December 24, 1741.

B. Elizabeth, daughter of George and Elizabeth Fawen, September 11, 1740.

M. John Fendall and Sarah Alexander, September 24, 1751.

M. Peter Fernandis and Mildred Gooly, July 29, 1792.

M. John Fewel and Mary Grigsby, October 14, 1726.

M. Sarah Fewel and Joseph Lee, July 22, 1792.

M. Ruth Finchum and John Pimm, December 29, 1760.

     FINDLESTON : FINGLESTON : FINLASON : FINLESON

B. Jane, daughter of Daniel and Margaret Finlason, February 26, 1737/8.

B. Margaret, daughter of Daniel and Margaret Finleson, November 3, 1742.

B. Lettice, daughter of Daniel and Margaret Finlason, September 25, 1744.

M. Daniel Findleston and Martha Whiting, February 10, 1755.

M. Jane Fingleson and Robert Rankins, December 26, 1756.

B. Robert, son of Mary Fingleston, August 14, 1760.

M. Mary Anne Findleston and John Addison, April 17, 1761.

B. William, son of John and Anna Barbara Fitzhugh, April 13, 1725.

B. Thomas, son of Henry and Susanna Fitzhugh, July 16, 1725.

B. Sarah, daughter of Major John and Anna Barbara Fitzhugh, April 30, 1727.

B. John, son of Henry and Susanna Fitzhugh, June 14, 1727.

B. [Torn]   John and Anna Barbara Fitzhugh, January [?], 1729/30.

B.. Betty, daughter of Colonel Henry and Lucy Fitzhugh, April 20, 1731.

B. William and Sarah, son and daughter of Henry and Susanna Fitzhugh,
     August 21, 1729.

B. Susanna, daughter of Captain Henry and Susanna Fitzhugh, September 19,
     1732.

D. Major John Fitzhugh, January 21, 1732/3.

B. Daniel, son of Major John and Anna Barbara Fitzhugh, June 27, 1733.

B. Anne, daughter of Colonel Henry and Lucy Fitzhugh, March 26, 1734.

M. Elizabeth Fitzhugh and Nathaniel Gray, August 12, 1734.

M. Sarah Fitzhugh and Edward Barradall, January 5, 1735/6.

B. Elizabeth, daughter of Captain Henry and Susanna Fitzhugh, August 23, 1736.

B. Lucy, daughter of Colonel Henry and Lucy Fitzhugh, October 26, 1736.

M. Barbara Fitzhugh of this Parish and the Reverend William McKay, Rector of Hanover Parish, February 6, 1738/9.

D. Anne, daughter of Colonel Henry Fitzhugh, October 1, 1739.

D. Lucy, daughter of Colonel Henry Fitzhugh, October 7, 1739.

M. Anne Fitzhugh of this Parish and the Reverend Robert Rose of St.Anne's Parish, November 6, 1740.

M. Anne Fitzhugh and William Allison, November 21, 1740.

B. William, son of Colonel Henry and Lucy Fitzhugh, August 24, 1741.

D. Colonel Henry Fitzhugh, December 6, 1742.

M. Betty Fitzhugh and Benjamin Grymes, February 12, 1746/7.

M. Sarah Fitzhugh and Francis Thornton, April 2, 1747.

M. Thomas Fitzhugh and Sarah Stuart, June 19, 1750.

B. George, son of Colonel Henry and Sarah Fitzhugh, January 15, 1756.

B. William Beverley, son of William and Ursula Fitzhugh, March 27, 1756.

M. Elizabeth Fitzhugh and William Thornton, April 26, 1757.

B. Daniel, son of William and Ursula Fitzhugh, March 15, 1758.

M. John Fitzhugh and Elizabeth Harrison, January 31, 1760.

B. Theodorick, son of William and Ursula Fitzhugh, July 20, 1760.

B. Thomas, son of Henry and Sarah Fitzhugh, March [blank], 1762.

M. Susanna Fitzhugh and Anthony Thornton, January 5, 1764.

B. Nicholas Battaile, son of Henry and Sarah Fitzhugh, May 10, 1764.

B. Philip, son of William and [blank] Fitzhugh, May 4, 1766.

M. Henry Fitzhugh and Elizabeth Stith, October 28, 1770.

M.   Daniel Fitzhugh and Susanna Potter, October 24, 1772.

M.   Sarah Fitzhugh and Theodorick Bland, December 5, 1772.

M.   Elizabeth Fitzhugh and Henry Fitzhugh, October 24, 1777.

M.   Lucy Fitzhugh and Alexander Campbell, December 3, 1788.

M.   Susannah Fitzhugh and Rice Wingfield Hooe, May 13, 1790.

M.   Jane Fitzhugh and Henry Dade Hooe, June 17, 1790.

D.   Mary, daughter of Rebecca Flagg, June 14, 1720.

D.   William Flagg, January 3, 1720/1.

M.   Jane Flagg and Samuel King, November 11, 1729.

B.   Joseph, son of Thomas and Sarah Fleeman [or Flecman], May 12, 1753.

M.   Thomas Fleeming and Frances Eaton, April 10, 1735.

B.   Elizabeth, daughter of Thomas and Frances Fleeming, December 15, 1735.

B.   Sarah, daughter of Thomas and Frances Fleeming, March 18, 1736/7.

M.   Thomas Fletcher and Mary Knight, March 2, 1742/3.

M.   Thomas Fletcher and Margaret Sharer, December 26, 1744.

M.   James Fletcher and Rachel Sebastian, April 21, 1745.

B.   Thomas, son of Thomas and Margaret Fletcher, December 20, 1745.

M.   Francis Fletcher and Lettice Spicer, November 8, 1745.

B.   James, son of James and Rachel Fletcher, June 18, 1746.

B.   Mary, daughter of Francis and Lettice Fletcher, August 21, 1746.

B.   Anne, daughter of James and Rachel Fletcher, August 26, 1748.

B.   Elizabeth, daughter of James and Rachel Fletcher, March 8, 1752.

M.   Thomas Fletcher and Margaret Hogsdale, March 29, 1752.

M.   Thomas Fletcher and Mary Jones, December 28, 1753.

B.   Mary, daughter of Thomas and Mary Fletcher, January 25, 1754.

M.   William Fletcher and Mary Grigsby, June 30, 1764.

B.   John Story, son of John and Margaret Flower, January 6, 1760.

B.   Margaret, daughter of John and Elizabeth Flower, August 25, 1765.

M.   Priscilla Flower and Alexander White, April 30, 1775.

FLOID : FLOYD

M.   Jasper Floid and Elizabeth Cupper, December 4, 1723.

B.   James, son of Jasper and Elizabeth Floid, August 15, 1725.

B.   Richard, son of Jasper and Elizabeth Floyd, [torn; circa 1728-1729].

B.   Margaret, daughter of Jasper and Elizabeth Floyd, November 13, 1732.

B.   John, son of Anne Floyd, May 17, 1742.

D.   Jasper Floyd, November 20, 1743.

M.   Anne Floyd and Thomas Williams, December 23, 1744.

M.   James Floyd and Margaret Lee, February 20, 1749/50.

M.   Helen Fog and John Conah, June 22, 1724.

M.   Anne Foly and Benjamin Grigsby, September 5, 1727.

D.   Richard Foote, March 21, 1724/5.

D.   Elizabeth Foote, April 1, 1725.

M.   Richard Foote and Katharine Fossaker, October 6, 1726.

M.   Hester Foote and John Grant, August 17, 1727.

B.   William, son of Richard and Katherine Foote, October 31, 1727.

D.   [Torn] Foote, June 7, 1729.

M.   George Foote of this Parish and Frances Berryman of Washington Parish,
     December 3, 1731.

B.   Sarah, daughter of Richard and Katherine Foote, January 29, 1732/3.

B.   George, son of George and Frances Foote, January 20, 1734/5.

B.   John, son of Richard and Katherine Foote, November 30, 1735.

B.   Gilson, son of George and Frances Foote, December 18, 1736.

B. Henry, son of Richard and Katherine Foote, April 11, 1738.

B. Katherine, daughter of Richard and Katherine Foote, November 24, 1740.

B. [Blank], son of Richard and Katherine Foote, October 3, 1743.

B. Elizabeth, daughter of Richard and Katherine Foote, December 10, 1746.

B. George, son of Richard Foote, March 6, 1749/50.

M. Sarah Foote and William Stuart, November 26, 1750.

D. Francis, son of Richard and Katherine Foote, October 12, 1753.

M. Catherine Foote and Lawrence Washington, October 5, 1774.

M. Richard Foote and Jane Stuart, December 16, 1795.

M. John Ford and Elizabeth Thornton, January 27, 1729/30.

B. Mary, daughter of John and Elizabeth Ford, March 6, 1731/2.

M. Warrener Ford of Washington Parish and Frances Seaton of this Parish, July 24, 1740.

M. Katharine Fossaker and Richard Foote, October 6, 1726.

M. Elizabeth Fountain and Simon Perry, February 16, 1791.

B. Chandler, son of Chandler and Mary Fowke, November 7, 1717.

B. Robert Dinwiddie, son of Gerard and Elizabeth Fowke, September 20, 1746.

M. Anne Fowke and John Hooe, March 14, 1755.

B. John, son of Gerard and Elizabeth Fowke, June 26, 1757.

M. Richard Fowke and Anne Bunbury, March 16, 1760.

B. Anne Harrison, daughter of C. and A. Fowke, September 13, 1760.*

B. Anphel, daughter of Gerard and Elizabeth Fowke, May 28, 1761.

B. Susanna, daughter of Richard and Anne Fowke, December [blank], 1761.

B. Frances, daughter of C. and Anne Fowke, May 15, 1762.*

* For some reason at the same time in 1770 Rev. William Stuart recorded the births of five of the children of Chandler Fowke (1732-1810) and Mary Harrison, his wife, who were married December 19, 1759 in Fauquier County, Virginia. Mr. Stuart errs in calling the mother of these children A(nne); she was Mary, daughter of Colonal Thomas Harrison (170? - 1774) and his wife née Ann Grayson.

52   SAINT PAUL'S PARISH REGISTER

M. Susanna Fowke and Henry Peyton, March 15, 1764.

B. George, son of Gerard and [blank] Fowke, April 10, 1764.

B. Caty, daughter of C. and A. Fowke, July 11, 1765.*

B. Nelly, daughter of Chandler and A. Fowke, January 19, 1768.*

B. Thomas Harrison, son of C. and A. Fowke, June 1, 1770.*

M. Judith Fowke and Enoch Berry, November 23, 1791. [King George County Marriage Register records license issued for this couple, May 11, 1790.]

M. Alice Fowler of Brunswick Parish and George Williams, December 31, 1734.

B. William, son of John and Elizabeth Fowler, December 22, 1774.

B. Susanna, daughter of John and Elizabeth Fowler, February 20, 1778.

B. Lucy, daughter of John and Elizabeth Fowler, May 19, 1782.

B. Augustus, son of John and Elizabeth Fowler, January 22, 1785.

M. Sarah Fox and Richard Chidley, December 21, 1722.

B. Mary, daughter of Martha Foye, February 19, 1750/1. #

D. John Frampton, a servant of Jeremy Crannidge, [torn], 1718.

D. Henry Francum, November 10, 1716.

D. Thomas Francome, a servant man belonging to Wilford Kelly, January 16, 1719/20.

D. Elizabeth Francam, January 4, 1727/8.

M. Sarah Frank of Washington Parish and John Baily, January 6, 1745/6.

M. Elizabeth Frank of Washington Parish and John Kendall, April 24, 1746.

M. William Frankam and Mary Kelly, June 22, 1728.

FRANKLIN : FRANKLING : FRANKLAN : FRANKLAND : FRANKLEN

M. John Frankling and Margaret Bowling, August 18, 1716.

B. John, son of John and Margaret Franklin, April 17, 1718.

B. John, son of John and Margaret Franklin, August 16, 1720.

* See footnote on page 51
# See Joy

B. Anne, daughter of Joseph and Sarah Frankland, October 5, 1745.

M. Cesar Franklin and Sarah Kitchin, August 28, 1746.

B. Polly, daughter of Cesar and Sarah Franklan, August 29, 1747.

B. John, son of Joseph and Sarah Franklen, January 18, 1747/8.

B. Winifred, daughter of Cesar and Sarah Franklan, September 16, 1748.

B. Sally, daughter of Cesar and Sarah Franklin, November 20, 1751.

M. Sarah Franklin and William Davis, May 13, 1752.

M. Samuel Franks and Parthenia Brown, January 19, 1786.

M. Martin Frayn and Mary Anderson, July 9, 1758.

B. Mary, daughter of Thomas and Frances Freeman, March 26, 1751.

M. Mason French and Margaret Lacy, April 16, 1749.

M. John French and Margaret Burgess, January 15, 1749/50.

M. Margaret French and Original Bowling, March 18, 1752.

M. [Blank] Friar and Jane Evans, December 1, 1769.

D. John Fruyn, September 25, 1728. *

M. Elizabeth Fruyn and Edward Clement, October 25, 1728.

M. Richard Fry and Margaret Hudson, July 11, 1745.

M. John Fullager and Mary Dart, January 26, 1761.

G

GEMERSEN : GEMERSON : GEMISON   SEE; JAMESON : JAMISON

M. Sarah Gardiner and Thomas Berry, October 21, 1784.

M. Winifred Garmony and Ignatius Haddock, October 20, 1729.

B. John, son of Anne Garree, October 26, 1748.

GARRAT : GARRATT : GARRET : GARRETT

M. William Garrett and Anne Chambers, January 28, 1717/8.

* This may be John Truyn; see page 144.

B. William and Jane, son and daughter of William and Anne Garratt, October 2, 1718.

D. Charles Garratt, May 12, 1722.

M. Mary Garret and John Hay, July 12, 1724.

D. Thomas Garret, October 18, 1735.

M. William Garret and Sarah Ambry, February 4, 1741/2.

B. John, son of William and Sarah Garret, March 14, 1745/6.

D. Sarah Garret, May 3, 1748.

B. Daniel, son of Daniel and Elizabeth Garret, January 11, 1762.

B. Frances Clifton, daughter of Daniel and Elizabeth Garrett, March 17, 1769.

B. Lewis, son of Nicholas and Martha George, April 16, 1727.

M. James Giles [or Gibs] and Nancy Oliver, March 24, 1788.

D. James Ginnis, May 20, 1718.

M. Jane Gladsteans and Peter Crafford, August 7, 1755.

M. Thomas Glover and Sarah Kelly, September 1, 1737.

B. John, son of Thomas and Sarah Glover, December 9, 1738.

B. Mary, daughter of Thomas and Sarah Glover, October 9, 1740.

B. Thomas, son of Thomas and Sarah Glover, April 18, 1743.

M. Sarah Glover and John Christie, August 28, 1743.

D. Thomas Glover, November 22, 1743.

M. William Goff and Mary Kelly, September 8, 1738.

B. Frances, daughter of William and Anne Goff, October 7, 1740.

M. [Blank] Goff and William Johnson, November 20, 1762.

M. Margaret Golding and John Bedford, August 8, 1729.

M. Thomas Golding and Frances Berry, January 28, 1738/9.

B. Mary, daughter of Sarah Gooden, January 19, 1741/2.

M. James Goodwin and Sarah Lawyer, June 5, 1735.

B. Barbara, daughter of James and Sarah Goodwin, February 15, 1735/6.

B. Elizabeth, daughter of James and Sarah Goodwin, January 10, 1739/40.

D. James Goodwin, February 15, 1739/40.

M. Mildred Gooly and Peter Fernandis, July 29, 1792.

M. Alexander Gordon and [mutilated]   1717.

M. John Gordon and Sarah Raddish, January 24, 1722/3.

M. Elizabeth Gordon and Griffin Johns, February 7, 1731/2.

M. Anne Gordon and John Oakly, February 14, 1744/5.

M. John Gordon and Elizabeth Musten, November 24, 1747.

B. Thomas, son of John Gordon, January 20, 1757.

B. William, son of John and Elizabeth Gordon, July 26, 1760.

B. George Meredith and Francis, sons of John Gordon, July 17, 1765.

M. John Gordon, Junior, and Margaret Rogers, November 22, 1776.

B. Robert, son of Ruben Gormack, March 3, 1744/5.

M. Penelope Gorman and Robert Barber, October 26, 1747.

M. Joseph Goss and Anne Joy, December 24, 1747.

B. Henry, son of Joseph and Anne Goss, October 27, 1761.

M. Henry Goss and Elizabeth Joy, August 8, 1773.

M. Mary Gosslen and Robert Crook, April 15, 1745.

M. Sophia Gotley and John Coggen, February 22, 1736/7.

M. James Gouch and Elizabeth Powers of Caroline County, February 21, 1762.

M. Nancy Gouldie and John Whiting, October 25, 1785.

    GRAFFORD : GRAFFORT   SEE: CRAFFORD : CRAFFORT

M. Sarah Graham and John Bryant, December 11, 1768.

M. John Grant and Hester Foote, August 17, 1727.

D. Mary Grant, November 22, 1729.

M. Andrew Grant and Mary Matthews, April 26, 1770.

M. Ann Mary Grant and William Matthews, December 5, 1781.

M. James Grant and Elizabeth Massey, January 10, 1793.

B. William, son of John and Elizabeth Gravat, January 31, 1731/2.

B. George, son of John and Elizabeth Gravat, July 26, 1733.

B. Katherine, daughter of John and Elizabeth Gravat, January 6, 1736/7.

B. Elizabeth, daughter of John and Elizabeth Gravat, February 7, 1739/40.

M. Elizabeth Gravat and James Mehorner, February 7, 1742/3.

M. John Gravat and Behethland Kelly, December 27, 1751.

B. Ursula, daughter of John and Behethland Gravat, June 10, 1752.

M. George Gravat and Catherine McCartie, May 9, 1756.

B. Ellis, son of George and Catherine Gravat, March 21, 1757.

M. Behethland Gravat and Alexander Jordan, October 30, 1758.

M. Elizabeth Gravat and Francis Selph, October 16, 1763.

M. Ursula Gravat and William McDonald, July 1, 1767.

M. Nathaniel Gray and Elizabeth Fitzhugh, August 12, 1734.

B. John, son of Nathaniel and Elizabeth Gray, May 9, 1735.

B. Mary, daughter of Nathaniel and Elizabeth Gray, November 1, 1736.

B. Nathaniel, son of Nathaniel and Elizabeth Gray, July 8, 1738.

B. Anna Barbara, daughter of Nathaniel and Elizabeth Gray, September 19, 1739.

B. Winifred, daughter of Nathaniel and Elizabeth Gray, October 5, 1741.

B. Nathaniel, son of Nathaniel and Elizabeth Gray, April 6, 1744.

B. George, son of Nathaniel and Elizabeth Gray, November 24, 1746 and died soon after.

Baptized Sarah, daughter of Nathaniel and Elizabeth Gray, February 6, 1747/8.

B. John, son of Nathaniel and Elizabeth Gray, April 25, 1750.

B. Margaret, daughter of Nathaniel and Elizabeth Gray, February 24, 1752.

B. George, son of George and Sarah Gray, August 10, 1756.

B. James, son of G. and Mary Gray, January 21, 1758.

M. John Gray and Sarah Thomas, May 11, 1758.

B. Francis, son of George and Mary Gray, October 22, 1759.

M. Winifred Gray and William Johnson, February 24, 1760.

B. Daniel, son of George Gray, December 9, 1761.

B. Elizabeth, daughter of John and Sarah Gray, April 15, 1762.

B. Nathaniel Weedon, son of George and [blank] Gray, October 19, 1763.

M. Sarah Gray and William Scott, April 18, 1765.

B. French, son of George and Mary Gray, March 11, 1766.

B. Peggy Strother, daughter of George Gray, July 20, 1768.

M. Mary Green of Washington Parish and James Yates of Sittenbourne Parish, November 19, 1745.

M. Thomas Green and Lydia Whitridge of Hanover Parish, March 24, 1745/6.

M. Catherine Greenleves and Edward Moring, October 16, 1779.

M. Martha Greenslet and Isaac Shepherd, February 17, 1749/50.

    GREGG   SEE: GRIGG : GRIGGS

M. John Ben Gregg and Sarah Smith, June 22, 1730.

D. Anne Gregg, February 9, 1730/1.

B. Mary, daughter of John Ben and Sarah Gregg, July 16, 1733.

M. George Gregg and Jane Vinson, February 5, 1734/5.

D. George Gregg, October 23, 1735.

B. Meriday, son of Ben John and Sarah Gregg, December 27, 1735.

M. Jane Gregg and Edmund Kelly, June 15, 1736.

B.   Sarah, daughter of John Ben and Sarah Gregg, January 6, 1736/7.

M.   Elizabeth Gregg and Richard Vincent, April 29, 1737.

B.   Samuel, son of John Ben and Sarah Gregg, May 6, 1739.

M.   William Griffin and Margaret Corbin, April 6, 1725.

M.   Elizabeth Griffin and James Berry, August 19, 1747.

M.   Sarah Griffin and James Newman, December 25, 1759.

M.   Anne Griffin and Thomas Sachary, April 21, 1760.

M.   Dully Griffin and John Acres, May 28, 1790.

B.   Katherine, daughter of Francis and Mary Griffith, December 1, 1726.

B.   John, son of Francis and Mary Griffith, October 30, 1731.

B.   Mary Anne, daughter of Richard and Jane Griffith, December 21, 1755.

M.   Mary Griffith and George Nailour Waple, July 26, 1792.

     GRIGG : GRIGGS   SEE: GREGG

B.   Mary, daughter of George and Eleanor Grigg, April 25, 1719.

B.   George, son of George and Eleanor Grigg, September 28, 1723.

B.   Elizabeth, daughter of George and Helenor Gregg, April 24, 1728.

M.   Elizabeth Griggs and William Young, August 29, 1746.

M.   George Griggs and Margaret Humfries, June 22, 1749.

B.   John, son of George and Margaret Grigg, August 25, 1750.

B.   Isabel, daughter of Jane Grigg, September 10, 1750.

M.   Elizabeth Griggs and John Christie, September 12, 1751.

B.   George, son of George and Jane Griggs, November 13, 1755.

B.   Eleanor, daughter of George and Margaret Griggs, March 5, 1758.

M.   Sarah Grigg and Charles Smith, January 20, 1759.

B.   Sarah, daughter of George and [blank] Griggs, August 5, 1760.

M.   Anne Griggs and Charles Smith, January 24, 1769.

M. Mary Griggs and Lewis Knowland, March 26, 1771.

M. Mary Grigsby and John Fewel, October 14, 1726.

M. Benjamin Grigsby and Anne Foly, September 5, 1727.

M. Margaret Grigsby and John Smith, November 5, 1728.

D. John Grigsby, supposed to be one hundred and seven years old, October 11, 1730.

M. Thomas Grigsby of Overwharton Parish and Anne Dishman of Washington Parish, November 25, 1729, by license.

M. Rose Grigsby and Benjamin Spicer, June 6, 1734.

M. James Grigsby and Sarah Sudduth, May 9, 1742.

M. Moses Grigsby of Overwharton Parish and Katherine Bransom, December 1, 1742.

B. Elizabeth, daughter of James and Sarah Grigsby, February 24, 1742/3.

D. Thomas Grigsby, May 7, 1745.

M. Rose Grigsby and Townshend Dade, December 12, 1745.

M. Rachel Grigsby and Isaac Rose, December 19, 1751.

M. Susannah Grigsby and Charles Stuart of King George County, November 9, 1752.

M. James Grigsby and Letitia Travers, January 18, 1753.

B. John, son of James and Sarah Grigsby, August 7, 1757.

M. Anne Grigsby and Samuel Grigsby, December 25, 1762.

M. Samuel Grigsby and Anne Grigsby, December 25, 1762.

M. Mary Anne Grigsby and John Markous, September 1, 1763.

M. Mary Grigsby and William Fletcher, June 30, 1764.

M. Jemima Grining and Stephen Cash, May 26, 1747.

M. James Grisset and Elizabeth Philips, May 19, 1791.

M. Benjamin Grymes and Betty Fitzhugh, February 12, 1746/7.

B. Benjamin, son of Benjamin and Betty Grymes, January 2, 1756.

M. Mary Grymes and William Randolph, May 18, 1770.

D. Elizabeth Gurly, November 10, 1726.

M. Thomas Guteridge and Sarah Rallings, May 16, 1782.

M. Anne Gutridge and Henry Smith, July 17, 1778.

M. James Gwatkin and Frances Dade, March 25, 1774.

H

M. Ignatius Haddock and Winifred Garmony, October 20, 1729.

B. Margaret, daughter of Ignatius and Winifred Haddock, February 10, 1731/2.

D. John Hadsworth, March 18, 1742/3.

B. Ann, daughter of Edward and Mary Hall, May 22, 1717.

D. Ann, daughter of Mary Hall, October 6, 1717.

B. Sarah, daughter of James and Catherine Hall, May 1, 1723.

Baptized Sarah, daughter of Joseph Hall and Mary Barron, November 8, 1725.

B. Katherine, daughter of James and Katherine Hall, June 3, 1726.

M. Joseph Hall and Mary Barron, October 13, 1727.

B. Billie, son of Elizabeth Hall, December 25, 1734.

D. Mary Hall, January 31, 1735/6.

D. Joseph Hall, February 9, 1735/6.

B. Frances, daughter of Bathsheba Hall, April 26, 1742.

B. Anne, daughter of Bathsheba Hall, April 11, 1744.

M. Michael Hall and Elizabeth Kelly, December 29, 1744.

M. Bathsheba Hall and Samuel McKee, March 5, 1744/5.

M. John Hall and Hannah Suddath, November 6, 1749.

M. Sarah Hall and Samuel Whiting, October 5, 1750.

B. Benjamin, son of John and Hannah Hall, November 14, 1751.

B. Anne, daughter of John and Hannah Hall, August 4, 1754.

B. Futral, son of Futral and Elizabeth Hall, April 14, 1760.

B. Hannah, daughter of Frances Hall, February 14, 1764.

M. John Hallet and Mary Walker, August 1, 1751.

D. Thomas Halsall, Commander of the Liverpool Merchant, September 25, 1738.

M. Margaret Hamilton and William Worton, February 26, 1724/5.

M. Elizabeth Ham and Thomas Hokins, July 24, 1716.

M. Thomason Ham and William Thomas, December 22, 1724.

M. Sarah Hamm and William Banton, December 1, 1730.

D. John Hamm, December 8, 1739.

HAMMAT : HAMMET : HAMMIT : HAMET : HAMIT

M. Daniel Hammat and Betridge Bowlin, November 2, 1728.

B. Violind, daughter of Daniel and Elizabeth Hammet, January 6, 1738/9.

B. Elizabeth, daughter of Daniel and Elizabeth Hammit, July 22, 1742.

B. Mildred, daughter of Daniel and Elizabeth Hammat, April 25, 1745.

M. John Hammet and Anne Donahoo, August 15, 1757.

B. George, son of Mildred Hammet, April 12, 1773.

M. Daniel Hamet and Eleanor Jones, December 22, 1774.

M. Anne Hamit and Zachariah Newble, November 6, 1779.

B. Elizabeth, daughter of John and Mary Hammond, October 12, 1772.

D. Joseph Hampton, February 20, 1725/6.

HANDLEY : HANDLY : HANLY : HENLY : HANDLEE

B. Bridget, daughter of Bryant and Sarah Henly, October 24, 1724.

D. Bridget Hanley, November 15, 1725.

M. Bryan Handley and Sarah Williams, December 28, 1726.

B. John, son of Bryant and Sarah Hanly, July 20, 1732.

62   SAINT PAUL'S PARISH REGISTER

D. Bryan Hanly, December 20, 1732.

M. Sarah Handly and Benjamin Lewis, August 31, 1734.

M. Margaret Handlee and Francis Mills, April 6, 1751.

B. John, son of Rachel Handly, September 24, 1746.

HANNIDGE : HANNIGE : HENNEAGE : HENNIDGE

D. Rebecca Hennidge, December 29, 1720.

B. Thomas, son of George and Elizabeth Hannidge, July 13, 1724.

D. Elizabeth, wife of George Hannidge, December 25, 1744.

B. Elizabeth, daughter of Thomas and Jane Hannidge, October 18, 1746.

B. Helenor, daughter of Thomas and Jane Hannige, August 22, 1748.

M. John Henneage and Molly Sparkes, October 22, 1785.

M. James Hansbury*and Lettice Sumner, September 19, 1741.

B. Mary, daughter of James Hansbury*, February 8, 1764 (Overwharton).

M. William Hansford and Sarah Doniphan, February 12, 1725/6, by license.

M. Benjamin Hansley and Elizabeth Hikkum, January 19, 1730/1.

M. William Hanson and Susanna Rorh, November 19, 1725.

M. George Hardin and Jane Bunbury, December 3, 1740.

M. Solomon Hardwick and Anne Peach, September 25, 1748.

M. John Harges and Elizabeth Luthrel, October 1, 1725.

B. Mildred, daughter of John and Elizabeth Harges, August 4, 1726.

M. Richard Harmon and Elizabeth Mizing of Washington Parish, March 28, 1746.

M. George Harris and Mary Carrol, July 14, 1750.

M. Elizabeth Harrison and Robert Dade, January 4, 1742/3.

M. Mary Harrison and George Catlett, November 23, 1758.

---

* Hansbury is an error for Hansbrough which is sometimes spelt Hansborough. James Hansbrough (circa 1719-1784) married Lettice Sumner; they lived in Overwharton Parish and that parish register contains an account of their children. The will of James Hansbrough is of record at Stafford County court.

M. Elizabeth Harrison and John Fitzhugh, January 3, 1760.

M. Benjamin Harrison and Mary Short, November 17, 1770.

M. John Harrod and Mary Ellis, August 4, 1728.

M. James Hartly and Mary Kelly, August 25, 1754.

M. James Hartly and Elizabeth Tilcock, April 1, 1768.

M. James Hartly and Anne Walpole, August 26, 1778.

M. Anne Hartly and Simon Perry, December 25, 1783.

M. Sarah Haukins and John Davis, August 7, 1750.

D. John Hawkins, November 20, 1717.

D. Christian Hawkins, November 12, 1721.

M. William Hawkins and Rose Cook, August 16, 1723.

D. Elizabeth Hawkins, June 30, 1726.

B. William, son of William and Rose Hawkins, October 3, 1727.

D. William Hawkins, September 14, 1734.

D. Thomas Hawkins, January 10, 1735/6.

M. Thomas Hawkins and Sarah Ancrum, July 13, 1746.

B. William, son of Thomas and Sarah Hawkins, April 17, 1747.

M. John Hay and Mary Garret, July 12, 1724.

B. Sarah, daughter of John and Mary Hay, May 19, 1725.

D. Sarah, daughter of John and Mary Hay, September 6, 1725.

B. Margaret, daughter of John and Mary Hay, October 18, 1732.

M. Mary Haydon and Peter Kilgore, November 1, 1722.

M. John Hayns and Margaret Linsy, September 8, 1728.

M. Sarah Head and William Dere, September 16, 1773.

M. Anne Heaps to William Skinner, August 20, 1767.

HENNEAGE : HENNIDGE   SEE: HANNIDGE : HANNIGE

B. Elizabeth, daughter of Thomas and Mary Heath, June 9, 1716.

B. Luke, son of Rose Heath, April 4, 1740.

B. George, son of Peter and Margaret Hedgman, December 11, 1735.

    HENNEAGE : HENNIDGE   SEE: HANNIDGE : HANNIGE

B. Winifred, daughter of Enoch and Elizabeth Hensley, February 25, 1752.

B. Robert, son of Osman and Alse Henvigh, in March and baptized April 8, 1716.

M. William Heselton and Hannah Leonard, July 7, 1765.

M. George Hibbill and Mary Triplett, February 12, 1728/9.

B. Lydia, daughter of John and Sarah Hickman, November 24, 1768.

M. Elizabeth Hikkum and Benjamin Hansley, January 19, 1730/1.

B. John, son of James and Catherine Higgins, May 17, 1716.

B. Jane, daughter of James and Catherine Higgins, December 4, 1719.

M. William Higgins and Sarah Newton, December 9, 1732.

M. John Hill and Elizabeth Mehony, October 1, 1716.

D. Elizabeth, daughter of John Hill, September 6, 1716.

B. Anne, daughter of John and Elenor Hill, December 25, 1717.

B. Mary, daughter of John and Elizabeth Hill, February 22, 1727/8.

M. Mary Hill and William Clift, January 19, 1730/1.

B. Sarah, daughter of John and Elizabeth Hill, January 24, 1730/1.

M. Frances Hill and Burdet Clifton, July 15, 1733.

B. Peggie, daughter of John and Elizabeth Hill, January 20, 1733/4.

M. Richard Hill and Sarah Burnsplat, December 22, 1737.

M. Mary Hilton and Carnaby Peyton, July 5, 1764.

B. Isobel, daughter of Archibald and Helenor Hodge, July 23, 1740.

B. Helen, daughter of Archibald and Helen Hodge, November 27, 1742.

M. Mary Hodge and Cochley [Colclough] Striblin, October 6, 1749.

M. Eleanor Hodge and Clement Sacheveral, November 8, 1763.

M. Isabel Hodge and Henry Butridge, December 30, 1764.

M. Nathaniel Hogdon and Margaret Oliver, March 2, 1746/7.

M. Margaret Hogsdale and Thomas Fletcher, March 29, 1752.

M. Thomas Hokins and Elizabeth Ham, July 24, 1716.

B. Lilly, daughter of James and Mary Holdan, March 1, 1759.

B. John, son of Tandy and Mary Holeman, July 14, 1731.

B. Anne, daughter of John and Anne Holland, May 12, 1752.

B. George, son of John and Elizabeth Holland, February 17, 1757.

B. Elizabeth, daughter of John and Elizabeth Holland, May 6, 1759.

M. Jane Holland and William Thompson, December 26, 1765.

M. Isabel Holland and Thomas Philips, June 14, 1772.

M. Elizabeth Holland and John Hudson, August 24, 1780.

M. Mary Holland and John Mildred Scott, February 26, 1784.

M. Anne Holloway and William Scapelan, September 29, 1748.

M. Elizabeth Holmon and Callohill Mennis, November 16, 1740.

B. Rice, son of Rice and Catherine Hooe, March 14, 1724/5.

D. Colonel Rice Hooe, April 19, 1726.

D. Frances Hooe, April 26, 1726.

M. Sarah Hooe and Philip Alexander, November 11, 1726.

M. John Hooe and Anne Alexander, November 23, 1726.

B. Richard, son of Rice and Katherine Hooe, October 15, 1727.

B. John, son of Howson and Anne Hooe, February 23, 1727/8.

D. Katherine Hooe, November 8, 1731.

B. Gerard, son of John and Anne Hooe, September 14, 1733.

B. Seymor, son of John and Anne Hooe, June 13, 1735.

SAINT PAUL'S PARISH REGISTER

B. Harris, son of Howson and Anne Hooe, January 1, 1735/6.

B. John, son of John and Anne Hooe, December 26, 1737.

B. Virolinda Harrison, daughter of Rice and Tabitha Hooe, February 28, 1738/9.

B. Bernard, son of Howson and Anne Hooe, October 30, 1739.

B. Anne, daughter of John and Anne Hooe, December 7, 1739.

B. Joseph Harrison, son of Rice and Tabitha Hooe, January 22, 1740/1.

B. Mary Townshend, daughter of Rice and Tabitha Hooe, February 27, 1741/2.

B. Sarah, daughter of John and Anne Hooe, March 7, 1741/2.

D. Parthenia, daughter of John and Anne Hooe, August 26, 1742.

B. William, son of Howson and Anne Hooe, September 9, 1743.

B. Robert Townshend, son of Rice and Tabitha Hooe, October 3, 1743.

B. Sarah, daughter of Rice and Tabitha Hooe, June 20, 1746.

M. Howson Hooe, Junior, and Mary Dade, September 26, 1746.

B. Henry Dade, son of Howson and Mary Hooe, June 9, 1747.

D. Mr. Rice Hooe, January 22, 1747/8.

B. Robert Howson, son of Howson and Elizabeth Hooe, November 22, 1748.

M. Frances Hooe and John Storke, March 21, 1750/1.

M. John Hooe and Anne Fowke, March 14, 1755.

B. Mary Ann, daughter of John Hooe, Junior, and Anne, his wife, November 7, 1756.

B. Rice Wingfield, son of Richard and Anne Hooe, June 25, 1764.

M. Sarah Hooe and Nathaniel Washington, December 17, 1767.

B. Sarah Barnes, daughter of Gerard and Sarah Hooe, June 5, 1769.

M. Bernard Hooe and Margaret Pratt, November 2, 1771.

M. Anne Hooe and William Allason, June 26, 1772.

M. Anne Hooe and Alvin Moxley, November 5, 1772.

M. Seymour Hooe and Sarah Alexander, March 9, 1776.

M. Susanna Hooe and Thomas Roy, September 7, 1777.

B. Nathaniel Harris, son of William and Anne Hooe, October 15, 1777.

B. Alexander Seymour, son of Seymour and Sarah Hooe, December 15, 1777.

B. Jane Seymour, daughter of Seymour Hooe, April 11, 1781.

M. Caty Hooe and William Winters, November 1, 1781.

M. William Hooe and Susanna Pratt, November 13, 1782.

M. Elizabeth Hooe and George Mason, April 22, 1784.

M. Rice Wingfield Hooe and Susanna Fitzhugh, May 13, 1790.

M. Henry Dade Hooe and Jane Fitzhugh, June 17, 1790.

B. Hannah Fitzhugh, daughter of Rice W. and Sukey Hooe, March 25, 1791.

D. William Hopkins, July 25, 1725.

B. Richard, son of Thomas Hornbuckle, September 4, 1764.

M. Mary Horsey and Thomas Dennet, June 18, 1758.

B. John and William, sons of Hugh and Elizabeth Horton, March 6, 1717/8.

M. William Horton of King George County and Mary Thornberry of Saint Paul's
    Parish, January 12, 1741/2.

M. Thomas Horton and Hannah Saunders, February 10, 1786. [King George Coun-
    ty Marriage Register gives the name of the bride as Hannah Sanders].

M. Sarah Howell and James McIntosh, December 17, 1773.

M. Margaret Hubart and John Travis, June 28, 1722.

    HUBBARD : HUBBUD : HUBUD

B. Elizabeth, daughter of Edward and Elizabeth Hubbard, July 4, 1716.

M. Moses Hubud and Sarah Lowry, March 23, 1726/7.

B. Edward, son of Moses and Sarah Hubbud, January 26, 1731/2.

M. Elizabeth Hubbud and James Bennet, December 10, 1731.

B. Sabrah, daughter of Moses and Sarah Hubbud, February 2, 1733/4.

B. Moses, son of Moses and Sarah Hubbud, March 18, 1735/6.

B. Sarah, daughter of Moses and Sarah Hubbud, November 1, 1738.

M. Mary Hudson and John Welch, November 16, 1727.

M. Margaret Hudson and Richard Fry, July 11, 1745.

M. John Hudson and Elizabeth Holland, August 24, 1780.

M. William Hudson and Margaret Rallins, March 10, 1785.

M. Mary Hudson and William Barrett, December 30,1785.

M. Luke Hughes and Behethland Kennedy, July 10, 1779.

D. Timothy Hughs, December 5, 1717.

D. Catherine, wife of Timothy Hughs, December 7, 1717.

HUMPHRIES : HUMPHREY : HUMPHREYS : HUMFRIES

B. John, son of John and Joyce Humphries, February 19, 1716/7.

B. William, son of John and Joyce Humphrey, December 6, 1720.

D. Richard, son of John and Joyce Humphreys, July 15, 1725.

D. Joseph Humphreys, January 22, 1725/6.

D. Katherine Humphreys, January 23, 1725/6.

M. Margaret Humfries and George Griggs, June 22, 1749.

B. Samuel, son of William and Sarah Humphrey, February 8, 1753.

HUMSTON : HUMSTONE

D. Mary Humstone, a child, January 19, 1725/6.

D. William Humstone, November 14, 1728.

D. Thomas Humston, December 1, 1730.

B. Thomas, son of Edward and Sarah Humston, March 17, 1731/2.

B. Anne, daughter of Edward and Sarah Humston, March 2, 1734/5.

B. Edward, son of Edward and Sarah Humston, September 22, 1737.

B. John, son of Edward and Sarah Humston, February 10, 1739/40.

B. Sarah, daughter of Edward and Sarah Humston, May 2, 1743.

B. William, son of John and Frances Humston, January 10, 1744/5.

M. Thomas Hungerford and Anne Washington, June 22, 1780.

D. Susanna Hurdly, February 9, 1725/6.

M. George Hutcheson and Mildred Wagstaff, September 19, 1727.

B. William, son of George and Mildred [? Hutcheson] [torn; circa 1728 -9].

B. [Blank], daughter of George and Mildred Hutcheson, June [blank], 1731.

B. Jane, daughter of George and Mildred Hutcheson, September 10, 1733.

D. George Hutcheson, January 26, 1734/5.

M. Mildred Hutcheson and Hugh Cannady, November 6, 1735.

M. Sarah Hutton and James Cullings, February 14, 1755.

M. John Hyatt and Anne Lloyd, January 7, 1717/8.

I

INGLES   SEE: ENGLES : ENGLIS

J

M. John Jackson and Rachel Rosser of Hanover Parish, January 31, 1731/2.

M. Samuel Jackson and Mary Delander, February 21, 1736/7.

B. James, son of Samuel and Mary Jackson, August 14, 1738.

D. Mary, wife of Samuel Jackson, December 1, 1739.

M. Samuel Jackson and Anne Berry, February 10, 1739/40.

B. Samuel, son of Samuel and Anne Jackson, May 16, 1742.

D. Anne, wife of Samuel Jackson, January 14, 1742/3.

D. Samuel Jackson, February 14, 1747/8.

M. Elizabeth Jackson and Henry Smith, July 11, 1753

M. Jane Jackson and Henry Bussey, November 21, 1758.

M. James Jackson and Mary Johnston, September 3, 1761.

B. Samuel, son of James and Mary Jackson, May 16, 1762.

M. Elizabeth Jackson and John Ashton, May 16, 1762.

M. James Jackson and Elizabeth Sweney, December 31, 1767.

B. Sarah, daughter of James and Elizabeth Jackson, April 1, 1768.

B. Elizabeth, daughter of James and Elizabeth Jackson, February 16, 1771.

B. Chandler, son of Samuel and Jane Jackson, April 3, 1772.

B. Anne, daughter of Samuel and Jane Jackson, May 26, 1774.

M. John James and Anne Sebastian, December 29, 1737.

B. Samuel, son of John and Anne James, November 19, 1738.

B. Sarah, daughter of John and Anne James, April 9, 1746.

M. John James and Anne Strother, September 16, 1763.

JAMISON : JEMISON : GEMERSEN : GEMERSON : GEMISON

D. Sarah Jemison, September 5, 1716.

M. William Gemison and Elizabeth Dalbin, December 30, 1725.

B. Mary, daughter of William and Elizabeth Gemersen, October 15, 1726.

B. Jarvis, son of William and Elizabeth Gemerson, April 26, 1728.

M. David Jamison and Jane Sebastian, May 7, 1744.

M. Thomas Jett and Lucinda Owens, January 12, 1775.

M. Griffin Johns and Elizabeth Gordon, February 7, 1731/2.

M. Margaret Johns and John Clift, March 2, 1738/9.

JOHNSON : JOHNSTON : JONSON

D. Sarah, daughter of William and Margaret Jonson, August 9, 1716.

B. Owen, son of Arthur and Rachel Johnson, August 27, 1716.

B. Christopher, son of William and Margaret Johnson, September 30, 1717.

D. Robert Johnson, May 21, 1718.

B. William, son of George and Jane Johnson, July 13, 1718.

B. Rachel Johnson's child, October 14, 1720.

D. Rachel Johnson, October 24, 1720.

D. Margaret Johnson, December 25, 1720.

D. Daniel Johnson, January 1, 1720/1.

B. Mary, daughter of George and Jane Johnson, January 30, 1720/1.

B. Alexander, son of George and Jane Johnson, April 5, 1723.

Baptized Sarah, daughter of Margaret Johnson, April 9, 1725.

M. Patrick Johnson and Sicily Duncan, November 17, 1724.

D. Margaret Johnson, January 6, 1725/6.

B. Charles, son of William and Mary Johnson, February 24, 1725/6.

M. Margaret Johnson and Thomas Lacy, April 30, 1726.

M. Patrick Johnson and Elinor Chambers, May 14, 1726.

D. George Johnson, October 26, 1726.

D. Thomas Johnson, October 26, 1727.

M. Elizabeth Johnson and Richard Lee, January 26, 1727/8.

M. Jacob Johnson and Helenor Delander, December 10, 1728.

M. Jane Johnson and Alexander Rigby, December 28, 1729.

M. John Johnson and Frances Powel, November 18, 1731.

B. William, son of John and Frances Johnson, August 16, 1732.

B. Elizabeth, daughter of Jacob and Helinor Johnson, April 16, 1733.

B. John, son of John and Frances Johnson, May 20, 1734.

M. George Johnson and Anne Cheesman, January 9, 1734/5.

B. Mary, daughter of John and Frances Johnson, December 7, 1735.

D. Mary Johnson, December 17, 1735.

B.   George, son of George and Anne Johnson, December 25, 1735.

B.   George, son of George and Anne Johnson, August 12, 1736.

B.   David, son of Sarah Johnson, January 18, 1737/8.

B.   [Blank], daughter of John and Frances Johnson, March 7, 1737/8.

B.   Lettice, daughter of John and Frances Johnson, April 6, 1738.

B.   Jane, daughter of Jacob and Helenor Johnson, August 14, 1738.

B.   James, a mulatto son of Mary Johnson, February 28, 1738/9.

B.   Jacob, son of Jacob and Helenor Johnson, April 3, 1741.

B.   Isabel, a mulatto daughter of Mary Johnson, May 30, 1742.

B.   John, son of John and Frances Johnson, December 5, 1742.

B.   William, son of George and Anne Johnson, January 21, 1742/3.

B.   Mildred, daughter of Jacob and Helenor Johnson, September 29, 1743.

M.   William Johnson and Mary Sebastian, January 5, 1743/4.

M.   Janet Johnson and Thomas Williams, November 13, 1744.

B.   John, son of William and Mary Johnson, March 24, 1743/4.

B.   Jane, daughter of William and Mary Johnson, June 1, 1746.

M.   Jacob Johnson and Margaret Regan, October 13, 1748.

B.   William, son of William and Mary Johnston, June 16, 1752.

M.   Jane Johnson and William Thomas, December 25, 1752.

M.   Lettice Johnson and Maxfield Whiting, February 3, 1753.

B.   Benjamin, son of Jacob and Margaret Johnston, April 3, 1755.

M.   Sarah Johnson and Henry Smith, Junior, March 19, 1756.

B.   Sukey, daughter of William Johnson, February 2, 1757.

B.   Margaret, daughter of William and Mary Johnson, January 10, 1757.

B.   William Sebastian, son of William and Mary Johnston, April 22, 1758.

B.   Charles, son of Jacob and Margaret Johnson, November 25, 1759.

M. William Johnson and Winifred Gray, February 24, 1760.

B. William, son of William and Winifred Johnson, October 15, 1760.

M. Mary Johnston and James Jackson, September 3, 1761.

M. William Johnson and [blank] Goff, November 20, 1762.

B. Anne, daughter of William and Frances Johnston, February 6, 1764.

B. Behethland, daughter of William and Frances Johnston, April 19, 1766.

B. Reuben, son of John and Jane Johnston, January 17, 1767.

B. Mary, daughter of Jacob and Sarah Johnston, April 29, 1767.

B. Frances, daughter of John and Mary Johnston, November 24, 1767.

M. Amelia Johnson and John Keith, January 5, 1768.

B. Mary Goff, daughter of William and Frances Johnson, February 11, 1769.

B. George, son of Jacob and Sarah Johnson, April 26, 1769.

B. Benjamin, son of Jacob and Sarah Johnson, December 25, 1771.

M. Frances Johnson and John Christy. January 20, 1771.

B. Margaret, daughter of John and Mary Johnson, February 21, 1771.

B. William, son of John and Mary Johnson, July 2, 1772.

B. Sarah, daughter of Jacob and Sarah Johnson, August 23, 1772.

M. John Johnston and Frances Dounton, July 30, 1778.

M. William Johnston and Patty Wharton, August 5, 1778.

M. Anne Johnston and Jacob Smith, November 1, 1781.

M. Mary Johnston and William Bennett, November 9, 1782.

M. Samuel Johnson and Peggy Birch, July 28, 1785.

M. Behethland Johnston and William Mitchel, September 4, 1787.

M. Sarah Jones and Richard Carver, January 21, 1722/3.

B. Charles, son of Henry and Anne Jones, September 14, 1725.

D. John Jones, January 19, 1725/6.

74

B. Frances, daughter of Mary Jones, April 6, 1732.

M. William Jones and Mary Baxter, July 26, 1744.

M. John Jones and Helenor Moss, August 16, 1744.

B. Thomas, son of William and Elister Jones, November 30, 1745.

B. Charles Calvert, son of John and Helenor Jones, June 4, 1746.

M. Matthew Jones and Rose Cavenoch, September 21, 1746.

B. Behethlem, daughter of John and Helenor Jones, July 14, 1748.

M. Anne Jones and William Lord, October 12, 1748.

M. William Jones and Elizabeth Alsop, February 9, 1749/50.

B. Nathaniel, son of John and Eleanour Jones, February 25, 1750/1.

B. Sarah, daughter of Frances Jones, March 7, 1752.

M. William Jones and Jane Reiney, April 20, 1752.

M. Frances Jones and Robert Rose, June 7, 1752.

B. Charles, son of John and Sarah Jones, February 24, 1753.

B. Mary, daughter of William and Elizabeth Jones, May 20, 1753.

B. Sebra, daughter of John and Eleanor Jones, October 7, 1753.

M. Mary Jones and Thomas Fletcher, December 28, 1753.

B. Anne, daughter of William and Elizabeth Jones, February 21, 1755.

B. John, son of Jane Jones, March 28, 1756.

B. Sukey, daughter of John and Alinda Jones, March 25, 1757.

B. Henry, son of Henry and Honor Jones, June 7, 1757.

B. Charles Buirn, son of Frances Jones, February 3, 1759.

M. Elizabeth Jones and David Parsons, February 25, 1759.

B. Jane, daughter of John and Eleanor Jones, March 16, 1762.

M. David Jones and Mary Boswell, February 18, 1763.

B. Benjamin, son of David and Anne Jones, April 18, 1767.

M. Behethland Jones and John Peed, February 14, 1770.

M. Joseph Jones and Mary Jordan of King George County, August 16, 1774.

M. Eleanor Jones and Daniel Hamet, December 22, 1774.

M. Sebry Jones and William Crank, February 8, 1778.

M. Jane Jones and Samuel Marshall, June 13, 1782.

M. James Jones and Mary Wilkerson, April 6, 1786. [King George County Marriage Register states the bride is a widow].

M. Susanna Jones and John Price, May 5, 1786. [King George County Marriage Register shows license issued to John Price, Junior, and Susanna Jones].

M. Nancy Jones and Richard Allen, February 4, 1788.

M. Mildred Jones and John Whiting, December 26, 1788.

B. Winifred, daughter of Elizabeth Jordan, October 4, 1745.

M. Elizabeth Jordan and William Ward, December 25, 1753.

M. Alexander Jordan and Behethland Gravat, October 30, 1758.

M. Esther Jordan and William Doick, December 20, 1762.

M. Mary Jordan of King George County and Joseph Jones, August 16, 1774.

D. William Joy, husband of Anne Joy, January 18, 1717/8.

B. William, son of Martha Joy, December 15, 1737.

B. Isaac, son of Martha Joy, December 30, 1743.

M. Anne Joy and Joseph Goss, December 24, 1747.

B. Anne, daughter of Martha Joy, April 5, 1748.

B. Mary, daughter of Martha Foye, February 19, 1750/1. [See page 52]

M. Anne Joy and Patrick Sheerman, August 9, 1768.

M. Isaac Joy and Elizabeth McCant, March 23, 1770.

B. William, son of Isaac and Elizabeth Joy, January 26, 1771.

M. Elizabeth Joy and Henry Goss, August 8, 1773.

K

M. Robert Kay and Elizabeth Strother, December 13, 1762.

M. Mary Kay and Enoch Strother, February 12, 1763.

B. Elizabeth, daughter of John and Elizabeth Keith, November 4, 1759.

B. Jane, daughter of John and Elizabeth Keith, July 2, 1764.

M. John Keith and Amelia Johnson, January 5, 1768.

M. Amie Keith and Peter Pluckett, December 27, 1775.

D. Lionel Kelly, August 10, 1717. ·

B. Elizabeth, daughter of Philip and Sarah Kelly, December 6, 1715.

D. Sarah Kelly, October 8, 1718.

B. Sarah, daughter of Wilford and Jane Kelly, November 10, 1721.

M. John Kelly and Jane Moss, December 21, 1722.

B. Elizabeth, daughter of John and Jane Kelly, [mutilated] 1723.

B. James, son of Alexander and Diana Kelly, November 30, 1725.

M. John Kelly and Mary Laton, December 4, 1725.

B. Jane, daughter of John and Mary Kelly, October 20, 1726.

M. Frances Kelly and Sylvester Moss, July 7, 1727.

B. Behethlem, daughter of John and Mary Kelly, March 30, 1728.

M. Mary Kelly and William Frankam, June 22, 1728.

B. Thomas, son of Wilford and Jane Kelly, [torn; circa 1728].

D. Wilford Kelly, August 24, 1728.

D. John Kelly, December 16, 1730.

B. Frances, daughter of John and Mary Kelly, April 10, 1731.

B. Anthony Buckner, son of Jane Kelly alias Thomas, April 30, 1731.

M. William Kelley and Margaret Dew of Hanover Parish, April 24, 1732.

M. Jane Kelly and Henry Smith, September 24, 1733.

M. Edmund Kelly and Jane Gregg, June 15, 1736.

B. Katherine, daughter of Edmund and Jane Kelly, March 4, 1736/7.

M. Sarah Kelly and Thomas Glover, September 1, 1737.

B. William, son of Mary Kelly, January 2, 1737/8.

M. Mary Kelly and William Goff, September 8, 1738.

B. John, son of Edmund and Jane Kelly, April 11, 1739.

B. Vinsen, son of Edmund and Jane Kelly, August 8, 1741.

M. Samuel Kelly and Behethlem White, August 25, 1741.

B. Wilford, son of Samuel and Behethlam Kelly, June 23, 1742.

M. Jane Kelly and Samuel Whiting, August 29, 1744.

B. Tabytha, daughter of Samuel and Behethlem Kelly, November 7, 1744.

M. Elizabeth Kelly and Michael Hall, December 29, 1744.

B. William, son of Thomas and Anne Kelly, April 11, 1745.

B. Charles, son of Margaret Kelly, April 30, 1746.

M. Elizabeth Kelly and Richard Dane, June 30, 1746.

M. Mary Kelly and William Lacy, December 4, 1746.

B. Sarah, daughter of Samuel and Behethlem Kelly, December 27, 1746.

B. Jasper, son of Thomas and Anne Kelly, February 21, 1746/7.

B. Edmund, son of Samuel and Behethlem Kelly, September 11, 1748.

M. William Kelly and Phillis McIntosh, August 22, 1751.

M. Behethland Kelly and John Gravat, December 27, 1751.

M. Mary Kelly and James Hartly, August 25, 1754.

B. Mary, daughter of William and Phillis Kelly, April 21, 1755.

M. James Kelly and Eleanor Burnsplat, April 15, 1757.

M. William Kelly and Jane Minor, March 30, 1758.

B. Isaac, son of William and Phillis Kelly, August 15, 1760.

M. Tabitha Kelly and Patrick Clarke, August 13, 1764.

M. Vincent Kelly and Elizabeth Sharp, January 26, 1769.

M. Woodford Kelly and Mildred Tunnel, February 4, 1769.

M. Winifred Kelly and Thomas Bateman, February 7, 1771.

M. Thomas Kelton and Margaret Skerry, December 24, 1726.

M. Joanna Kemmet and Joseph Lane, May 22, 1754.

M. John Kendall of Washington Parish and Frances Sharp of this Parish, December 22, 1737.

B. Thomas, son of John and Frances Kendall, December 1, 1738.

M. John Kendall and Elizabeth Frank of Washington Parish, April 24, 1746.

B. Molly, daughter of George and Margaret Kendall, May 2, 1757.

M. John Kennedy and Rose Sudduth, June 21, 1736.

B. Mildred, daughter of Hugh and Mildred Kennedy, May 22, 1736.*

B. Isaac, son of William and Margaret Kennedy, June 12, 1758.

M. Thomas Kennedy and Frances Lucas, October 9, 1763.

M. Behethland Kennedy and Luke Hughes, July 10, 1779.

M. Martha Kenneman and John Sutton, September 17, 1723.

M. Michael Kenny and Margaret Bignell, July 29, 1750.

M. Peter Ker and Sarah Stribling, August 23, 1728.

M. Sarah Ker and Charles Martin, October 1, 1736.

B. John, son of Jeremiah and Anne Kersey, March 20, 1758.

D. John Kidwell, June 16, 1725.

M. Elizabeth Kidwell and William Bowline, September 7, 1726.

M. Mary Kidwell and Samuel Thornbery, April 20, 1744.

M. Peter Kilgore and Mary Haydon, November 1, 1722.

---

*   See page 23 under Cannady for marriage of this couple.

D. William King, December 21, 1726.

M. Robert King and Margaret Sebastian, April 26, 1727.

D. Joseph King, Senior, September 26, 1728.

M. Samuel King and Jane Flagg, November 11, 1729.

B. Joshua, son of Robert and Margaret King, January 3, 1730/1.

B. Joseph, son of Joseph and Sarah King, February 21, 1731/2.

B. Sarah, daughter of Samuel and Jane King, March 29, 1732.

M. Joseph King and Sarah Carrico, May 7, 1731.

B. Anne, daughter of Robert and Margaret King, July 16, 1733.

B. Jane, daughter of Samuel and Jane King, August 12, 1733.

B. Joel, son of Joseph and Sarah King, May 10, 1734.

M. William King and Mary Trigger, August 2, 1735.

B. William, son of Robert and Margaret King, May 29, 1736.

B. Nimrod, son of William and Mary King, October 29, 1736.

B. Susanna, daughter of Joseph and Sarah King, December 18, 1736.

B. Robert, son of Robert and Mary King, April 18, 1739.

B. Mary, daughter of Joseph and Sarah King, May 2, 1739.

B. Benjamin, son of Robert and Mary King, November 19, 1741.

B. Isaac, son of Robert and Mary King, November 17, 1745.

M. Thomas King and Jane Thomas, May 19, 1771.

B. William, son of Richard and Jane King, June 12, 1772.

M. Sarah Kirk and William Bowline, June 24, 1726.

M. Hezekiah Kirk and Behethland Bennet, February 10, 1778.

M. Jeremiah Kirk and Ann Monroe, August 18, 1785.

KITCHEN : KITCHIN : KITCHING

D. Thomas Kitchen, March 20, 1715/6.

M. Anthony Kitchen and Mary Overall, August 31, 1727.

B. Sarah, daughter of Anthony and Mary [? Kitchen], [torn; circa 1728-1729].

B. William, son of Anthony and Mary Kitchen, February 23, 1731/2.

B. Mary, daughter of Anthony and Mary Kitchen, November 14, 1734.

B. Anthony, son of Anthony Kitchen, August 22, 1736.

B. Jane, daughter of Anthony and Mary Kitchen, January 26, 1738/9.

B. George, son of Anthony and Mary Kitchen, May 16, 1741.

B. Elizabeth, daughter of Anthony and Mary Kitchen, August 20, 1743.

B. Anthony, son of Sarah Kitchen, November 7, 1745.

M. Sarah Kitchen and Cesar Franklin, August 28, 1746.

D. Anthony Kitchen, March 17, 1746/7.

B. Peggy, daughter of Anthony and Mary Kitchen, June 28, 1747.

M. Mary Kitchen and John Lewright, August 8, 1751.

M. Elizabeth Kitchen and Joseph Lacy, September 10, 1759.

B. James, son of Thomas and Mary Kitchen, October 4, 1756.

B. William, son of Thomas and Elizabeth Kitchen, October 14, 1756.

B. Thomas, son of Anthony and Sarah Kitchen, January 4, 1760.

B. Sukey, daughter of Anthony and [blank] Kitchen, March 1, 1763.

B. George Monroe, son of Anthony Kitchen, February 7, 1766.

B. Sarah, daughter of Anthony and Sarah Kitchen, December 11, 1771.

B. Jane, daughter of Anthony and Sarah Kitchen, June 4, 1772.

D. William Knight, son of Catherine Moss, April 2, 1717.

M. William Knight and Jane Butler, December 26, 1734.

M. Jane Knight and John Demsoe, July 6, 1737.

M. Mary Knight and Thomas Fletcher, March 2, 1742/3.

M. Lewis Knowland and Mary Griggs, March 26, 1771.

M. John Knowling and Mildred Stribling, April 11, 1776.

                                    L

M. John Lacky and Sarah Payn, June 6, 1737.

M. Thomas Lacy and Judith Rawlins, November 9, 1716.

B. John, son of Thomas and Judith Lacy, October 30, 1717.

B. Anne, daughter of Thomas and Judith Lacy, January 28, 1720/1.

B. Thomas, son of Thomas and Judith Lacy, February 19, 1723/4.

D. Lucia Lacy, November 11, 1725.

B. William, son of Thomas and Sarah Lacy, December 5, 1725.

M. Thomas Lacy and Margaret Johnson, April 30, 1726.

B. Sarah, daughter of Thomas and Margaret Lacy, May 6, 1731.

B. Jacob, son of Thomas and Margaret Lacy, January 2, 1733/4.

B. Joseph, son of Thomas and Margaret Lacy, January 25, 1736/7.

D. John, son of Thomas Lacy, December 5, 1739.

M. William Lacy and Mary Kelly, December 4, 1746.

B. Anne, daughter of William and Mary Lacy, April 16, 1747.

B. John, son of William and Sarah Lacy, September 3, 1748.

M. Margaret Lacy and Mason French, April 16, 1749.

M. Mary Lacy and Thomas Paremane, August 28, 1751.

M. Joseph Lacy and Elizabeth Kitchen, September 10, 1759.

B. Thomas, son of Joseph and Elizabeth Lacy, January 1, 1764.

M. Anne Lambert and John Wilson, October 28, 1759.

B. Mary, daughter of William and Sarah Lampton, June 30, 1734.

B. William, son of John and Catherine Land, April 9, 1771.

B. Elisha, son of Elizabeth Land, November 28, 1772.

D. James Landen, March 21, 1731/2.

M. Joseph Lane and Joanna Kemmet, May 22, 1754.

LATHAM : LATHRAM : LATHRUM : LATHUM

M. Mary Lathram and Benjamin Bowline, July 27, 1725.

B. Sarah, daughter of John and Mary Lathrum, February 24, 1725/6.

B. Franklin, son of John and Mary Latham, March 26, 1728.

B. Snadwell, son of John and Mary Lathrum, January 24, 1730/1.

B. Hannah, daughter of Stephen and Joanna Lathum, April 19, 1739.

M. Mary Laton and John Kelly, December 4, 1725.

M. Joshua Lawyer and Sarah Neal, June 24, 1732.

D. Joshua Lawyer, March 13, 1733/4.

D. John Lawyer, March 19, 1733/4.

M. Sarah Lawyer and James Goodwin, June 5, 1735.

D. Edward Lawyer, January 17, 1739/40.

M. Sarah Ledrim to Henry Lock, September 17, 1722.

M. Richard Lee and Margaret Brady, July 8, 1723.

M. Richard Lee and Elizabeth Johnson, January 26, 1727/8.

D. Richard Lee, Senior, April 4, 1731.

B. Mildred, daughter of Richard and Elizabeth Lee, August 2, 1731.

M. Lettice Lee and John Corbin, September 1, 1737.

B. Anne, daughter of Richard and Elizabeth Lee, April 2, 1738.

D. Margaret, widow of Richard Lee, February 9, 1739/40.

B. Bennet, son of John and Sarah Lee, February 24, 1739/40.

B. Sarah, daughter of Richard and Elizabeth Lee, December 30, 1741.

D. Elizabeth Lee, July 4, 1743.

M. Richard Lee and Mary Rose, June 29, 1744.

B. William, son of John and Sarah Lee, October 20, 1744.

M. Margaret Lee and James Floyd, February 20, 1749/50.

M. John Lee and Fanny Underwood, March 2, 1790.

M. Joseph Lee and Sarah Fewel, July 22, 1792.

M. Sarah Leech and Henry Smith, December 29, 1767.

LIFTIDGE : LEFTWIDGE

B. Elisha, son of Thomas and Rosamond Leftidge, June 18, 1738.

B. Mary, daughter of Elisha and Priscilla Leftidge, September 2, 1742.

B. Anne, daughter of Elisha and Priscilla Leftidge, October 22, 1744.

B. Susanna, daughter of Elisha and Priscilla Leftwidge, October 6, 1746.

B. Rosamond, daughter of Elisha and Priscilla Leftwidge, August 22, 1748.

M. Elizabeth Leg and Rehobeth Barnfather, December 21, 1724.

D. Mary Lennard, December 29, 1717.

D. John Lenpey [?], December 18, 1717.

M. Hannah Leonard and William Heselton, July 7, 1765.

LEVEE : LEVI : LEVY

B. Alice, daughter of Abraham and Anne Levee, September 28, 1748.

B. Jacob, son of Abraham and Anne Levy, October 23, 1759.

B. John, son of Frances Levy, February 25, 1773.

M. Sarah Levi and William Trigger, February 1, 1786.

M. Mary Lewis and James Power, October 19, 1724.

M. Thomas Lewis and Elizabeth Mealy, October 5, 1730.

B. Daniel, son of Thomas and Elizabeth Lewis, October 14, 1733.

M. Benjamin Lewis and Sarah Handly, August 31, 1734.

D. Benjamin Lewis, September 2, 1735.

M. Sarah Lewis and Leonard Martin, November 27, 1736.

M. Elizabeth Lewis and William Lord, October 23, 1738.

M. Daniel Lewis and Elizabeth Rose, August 31, 1762.

B. Thomas, son of Daniel and Elizabeth Lewis, April 2, 1764.

B. Benjamin, son of Benjamin and Elizabeth Lewis, April 17, 1769.

M. Elizabeth Lewis and Benoni Stratton, September 29, 1772.

M. Clarinda Lewis and Isaac Rodgers, December 11, 1791.

M. John Lewright and Mary Kitchen, August 8, 1751.

M. John Limit and Anne Bateman, April 6, 1751.

B. Elizabeth, daughter of John and Anne Limit, September 10, 1753.

B. George, son of John and Anne Limit, July 16, 1755.

M. Elizabeth Limmit and James Buchanan, December 7,1777.

LINDLY : LINEY : LINSEY : LINSY : LINZIE   [LINDSAY ? LINDSEY]

B. Anne, daughter of Dennis and Barbara Linsey, October 14, 1725.

B. Moses, son of Dennis and Barbara Linzie, January 31, 1727/8.

M. Margaret Linsy and John Hayns, September 8, 1728.

B. Anne, daughter of Dennis and Elizabeth Linsey, January 20, 1730/1.

B. Wilkison, daughter of Denise and [blank] Linsey, July 20, 1733.

B. Sarah, daughter of Denis and [blank] Liney, February 10, 1735/6.

B. Denis, son of Denis and Barbara Linsey, May 8, 1738.

M. John Linsey and Sarah Clift, January 3, 1739/40.

M. Barbara Linsey and Josiah Bransam, August 5, 1742.

M. Robert Lindly and Anne McLeod, August 21, 1744.

B. Winifred, daughter of Matthew and Anne Linsy, April 14, 1746.

M. Ambrose Lipscomb and Winifred Mardus, December 23, 1785.

M. Anne Lloyd and John Hyatt, January 7, 1717/8.

M. Jasper Lloyd and Anne Chambers, January 7, 1717/8.

M. Sarah Lloyd and William Dick, July 25, 1732.

D. Benjamin Lloyd, January 15, 1736/7.

M. Henry Lock and Sarah Ledrim, September 17, 1722.

M. Henry Lock and Elizabeth Blackman, February 6, 1724/5.

M. William Long and Eleanor Bolton, May 15, 1749.

B. Sarah, daughter of William and Anne Long, May 2, 1753.

B. Elizabeth, daughter of William and Anne Long, February 18, 1756.

B. Anne, daughter of William and Mary Long, April 8, 1758.

B. David, son of William and Anne Long, July 5, 1760.

B. Mary, daughter of William and Anne Long, July 8, 1762.

M. Elizabeth Long and John Tunnel, February 13, 1774.

M. William Long and Joanna Chivrel, December 30, 1790.

M. William Lord and Elizabeth Lewis, October 23, 1738.

B. William, son of William and Elizabeth Lord, January 12, 1738/9.

D. Elizabeth Lord, September 3, 1741.

M. William Lord and Clary Mannard, January 8, 1741/2.

B. Robert, son of William and Clary Lord, October 5, 1747.

M. William Lord and Anne Jones, October 12, 1748.

B. William, son of William and Anne Lord, April 9, 1756.

M. William Lord and Frances Stratton, October 31, 1756.

B. Benjamin, son of William and Frances Lord, March 15, 1757.

B. Clary, daughter of William and Ann Lord, January 12, 1762.

B. Elisha, son of William and Frances Lord, August 10, 1766.

B. Lucy, daughter of William and Frances Lord, January 10, 1769.

B. Frances, daughter of William and Frances Lord, February 15, 1771.

B. Willoughby, son of William and Frances Lord, May 7, 1772.

M. William Lord and Nelly Wilson, April 7, 1780.

M. John Lowry and Elizabeth Seaton, April 23, 1726.

M. Sarah Lowry and Moses Hubud, March 23, 1726/7.

D. Elizabeth Lowry, March 25, 1733.

B. Elizabeth, daughter of Thomas and Elizabeth Lowther, April 15, 1726.

M. Anthony Lucas and Sarah Stransford, November 4, 1737.

B. Anne, daughter of Anthony and Sarah Lucas, January 7, 1737/8.

B. Augustin, son of Anthony and Sarah Lucas, September 6, 1743.

B. Frances Lucas, January 2, 1743/4.

B. Annanah, a mulatto daughter of Frances Lucas, April 2, 1747.

M. Anne Lucas and Thomas Evans, February 4, 1753.

B. Anne, a mulatto daughter of Sarah Lucas, November 16, 1753.

B. Anthony Lucas, a mulatto, January 21, 1757.

M. Frances Lucas and Thomas Kennedy, October 9, 1763.

B. Mark, son of Sarah Lucas, August 5, 1764.

B. Anthony, son of Francis [? Frances] Lucas, June 6, 1772.

B. Susanna, daughter of Sarah Lucas, March 13, 1774.

B. Henry, son of Sarah Lucas, August 3, 1784; "to be free at twenty one".

D. Mrs. Frances Lund, daughter of Capt Lund, deceased, October 19, 1716.

M. Elizabeth Lund and Townshend Washington, December 22, 1726.

M. Elizabeth Luthrel and John Harges, October 1, 1725.

M. Timothy Lyons and Sarah Sebastian, January 11, 1746/7.

Mc

M. Mary McBean and John Whiting, August 10, 1791. [King George County Marriage Register gives the name of the bride as Mary Mackbaine].

M. Jane McCant and Thomas Carrico, October 4, 1744.

M. James McCant and Elizabeth Walker, March 15, 1747/8.

B. Elizabeth, daughter of James and Elizabeth McCant, December 27, 1748.

B. Joseph, son of James and Elizabeth McCant, October 15, 1751.

B. James, son of James and Elizabeth McCant, December 17, 1753.

B. Sally, daughter of James and Elizabeth McCant, August 17, 1757.

B. James, son of James and Elizabeth McCant, September 22, 1762.

M. Elizabeth McCant and Isaac Joy, March 23, 1770.

B. Dorothy, daughter of Margaret McCarty, July 8, 1724.

D. Robert McCarty, January 27, 1725/6.

M. Winifred McCarty and Robert Massey, December 20, 1728.

M. [Multilated] ho.^{S} McCarty and Grisel Matthew, December 23, 1728.

M. Hugh McCarty and Helenor Sulyvan, April 22, 1730.

D. Mrs. Anne McCarty, January 12, 1731/2.

B. Sarah McCarty, a mulatto, September 3, 1732.

D. Sarah McCarty, a mulatto child, October 17, 1732.

B. William, son of Mary McCarty, February 3, 1733/4.

B. Katherine, daughter of Margaret McCarty, March 19, 1735/6.

M. Margaret McCarty and Henry Bussey, July 11, 1741.

M. Catherine McCartie and George Gravat, May 9, 1756.

M. Daniel McCarty and Mary Mercer, April 3, 1764.

M. Daniel McCarty and Winifred Thornton, January 13, 1765.

B. James, son of Anne McCleaning, March 12, 1732/3.

M. John McCormick and Elizabeth Suttle of Hanover Parish, March 8, 1735/6.

M. Reverend Roderick McCulloh and Elizabeth Weedon of Washington Parish, February 17, 1734/5.

D. James McCulloh, December 12, 1735.

B. Winifred, daughter of James and Anne McDaniel, April 2, 1748.

M. James McDonald and Martha Withers of Overwharton Parish, November 15, 1732.

M. Edward McDonald and Elizabeth Smith, February 6, 1735/6.

M. Mary McDonald and John Alsop, August 20, 1737.

M. Alinda McDonald and Benjamin Wilson, February 27, 1757.

B. Jane and Margaret, daughters of Briant and Judith McDonald, January 30, 1760.

M. William McDonald and Ursula Gravat, July 1, 1767.

M. Jane McDonald and David Briggs, June [blank], 1771.

M. James McDuff and Mary Walker, March 3, 1757.

M. Anne McFarlan and William Scipier, February 17, 1750/1.

D. Mr. David McGill, November 5, 1725.

D. Sarah McGill, Gentlewoman, November [blank], 1749.

B. Mary, daughter of John and Margaret McGilvray, September 14, 1739.

M. Malcolm McIntosh and Mary Wood, November 24, 1743.

B. Peggie, daughter of James and Phillis McIntosh, November 10, 1748.

B. James, son of James McIntosh, January 30, 1750/1.

M. Mary McIntosh and Clement Shevry, August 11, 1751.

M. Phillis McIntosh and William Kelly, August 22, 1751.

M. James McIntosh and Sarah Howell, December 17, 1773.

M. The Reverend Mr. William McKay, Rector of Hanover Parish, and Barbara Fitzhugh of this Parish, February 6, 1738/9. [The marriage was announced in the Virginia Gazette, published in Williamsburg, March 2, 1738/9; it stated the bride was the daughter of "Major John Fitzhugh of Stafford County, deceased, a young Lady of great Beauty and Merit."]

MACKAY : MACKEE : MACKIE : MCKEE : MCKEY   SEE: MCKAY Page 88

B. Elizabeth, daughter of James and Sarah McKey, November 5, 1720.

D. Sarah McKey, November 15, 1720.

D. Elizabeth, daughter of James and Sarah McKey, deceased, January 25, 1720/1.

D. James McKey, April 17, 1733.

B. Sarah, daughter of John and Margaret MacKay, April 23, 1738.

M. Anne McKey and Thomas Emmerson, April 17, 1743.

M. Samuel McKee and Bathsheba Hall, March 5, 1744/5.

B. John, son of Samuel and Bathsheba MacKie, free mulattoes, November 23, 1745.

B. Elijah, a mulatto son of Samuel and Bathsheba MacKie, August 25. 1748.

B. Jane, daughter of Samuel and Bathsheba McKee, February 2, 1752.

B. Thomas, son of Margaret McKee, March 4, 1764.

B. Mary, daughter of Margaret McKee, August 10, 1767.

B. Margaret, daughter of Anne McKinnen, March 15, 1753.

M. Richard McLachlan and Elizabeth Smith, January 31, 1760.

B. Jane, daughter of Richard and Elizabeth McLachlan, October 9, 1762.

M. John McLean and Helenor Bell, April 14, 1745.

M. Anne McLeod and Robert Lindly, August 21, 1744.

M

M. John MacClanin and Elizabeth Barker, March 24, 1793.

M. Sarah Macnall and Samuel Sims, July 10, 1735.

M. Mary Maddox and John Curley, May 9, 1767.

MAHONEY : MAHONY : MEHONY : MEHONEY : MEHORNER : MEHORNEY

M. Elizabeth Mehony and John Hill, October 1, 1716

B. Mary, daughter of Dennis and Mary Mahony, April 29, 1725.

B. Dennis, son of Dennis and Rebecca Mahony, March 29, 1728.

B. William, son of Dennis and Rebecca Mahony, March 15, 1731/2.

B. Elizabeth, daughter of Dennis and Rebecca Mahony, August 20, 1736.

B. Benjamin, son of Dennis and Rebecca Mehony, January 24, 1738/9.

D. Dennis Mahony, September 23, 1740.

B. John, son of Dennis and Rebecca Mahony, May 26, 1741.

M. James Mehorner and Elizabeth Gravat, February 7, 1742/3.

B. Sarah, daughter of James and Elizabeth Mehorner, April 15, 1743.

D. Sarah Mehoney, November 22, 1744.

B. Denis, son of James and Elizabeth Mehorner, December 9, 1745.

B. James, son of James and Elizabeth Mehorner, January 19, 1748/9.

M. William Mehony and Rebecca Oliver, September 15, 1759.

B. Benjamin, son of Dennis and Margaret Mehony, October 24, 1759.

B. Henry, son of Dennis and Margaret Mehorner, September 12, 1761.

M. Dennis Mehorner and Jane Carver, September 8, 1766.

B. John, son of Dennis and Margaret Mehorner, July 7, 1768.

B. Elizabeth, daughter of Dennis and Jane Mehorner, September 12, 1772.

B. James, son of Dennis and Jane Mehorner, March 24, 1774.

M. Benjamin Mehorner and Margaret Noting, April 5, 1778.

M. Dennis Mehorner and Sarah Thompson, February 21, 1781.

M. Thomas Mehorner and Bethia Evans, March 30, 1786.

M. Henry Mehorner and Leah Skinner, September 13, 1788. [King George County
    Marriage Register gives the name of the bridegroom as Henry Mahorney].

M. Benjamin Mehorner and Elizabeth Wiggins, October 24, 1790. [King George
    County Marriage Register gives the name of the bridegroom as Benjamin
    Mahorney].

M. Eli Mehorney and Letty Owens, June 23, 1792.

MANING : MANNAN : MANNARD : MANNOR : MANWOOD

M. Robert Mannard and Clary Derrick, May 27, 1723.

D. Elizabeth, daughter of Robert and Clary Mannor, September 6, 1725.

B. Clary, daughter of Robert and Clary Manwood, July 12, 1726.

B. William, son of Robert and Clary Maning, April 15, 1732.

B. John and Robert, sons of Robert and Clary Mannard, November 6, 1734.

B. Derrick, son of Robert and Clary Mannard, November 1, 1737.

M. Clary Mannard and William Lord, January 8, 1741/2.

M. William Mannan and Martha Davis, August 13, 1752.

M. Keziah Mannard and Benjamin Trusloe, March 12, 1786. [King·George County Marriage Register gives the name of the bride as Keziah Mannan].

M. Clary Mannard and William Richardson, January 16, 1791. [King George County Marriage Register gives the name of the Bride as Clary Manning].

M. Amie Mannard and Aaron Owens, May 13, 1791.

M. Elizabeth Mardus and Joseph Rallins, May 25, 1778.

M. Aaron Mardus and Mary Thomas, March 12, 1785.

M. Winifred Mardus and Ambrose Lipscomb, December 23, 1785.

M. Elizabeth Mardus and Robert Alsop, January 3, 1791.

M. Moses Mardus and Mary Price, February 27, 1791. [King George County Marriage Register gives the name of the bridegroom as Marders].

M. Elizabeth Mardus and Bartlett White, March 2, 1792.

M. John Markous and Mary Anne Grigsby, September 1, 1763.

B. Anne, daughter of John and Elizabeth Marshall, April 29, 1726.

D. Anne, widow of Thomas Marshall, March 28, 1740.

M. Rush Marshall and Joanna Pede, November 23, 1779.

M. Samuel Marshall and Jane Jones, June 13, 1782.

M. Anne Martin and Joseph Sebastian, February 6, 1717/8.

B. Rose, daughter of Leonard and Sarah Martin, November 3, 1718.

B. Ann, daughter of Leonard and Sarah Martin, June 3, 1722.

B. John, son of Leonard and Sarah Martin, [mutilated - ? 1724/5 ?].

B. Leonard, son of Leonard and Sarah Martin, July 14, 1726.

M. Charles Martin and Sarah Ker, October 1, 1736.

M. Leonard Martin and Sarah Lewis, November 27, 1736.

B. Anne, daughter of Leonard and Sarah Martin, August 24, 1738.

M. John Martin and Lucy Todd, November 5, 1742.

D. John Martin, November 24, 1742.

B. Leonard, son of Leonard and Sarah Martin, March 17, 1742/3.

B. James, son of Lucy Martin, May 22, 1744.

B. Sarah, daughter of Leonard and Sarah Martin, July 10, 1746.

M. Sarah Martin and Alexander Douglas, September 8, 1751.

M. Anne Martin and Thomas Mustin, January 19, 1759.

M. Sarah Martin and John Tunnel, February 18, 1763.

M. Leonard Martin and Elizabeth More, December 28, 1764.

B. William, son of Leonard and Mary Martin, December 31, 1772.

M. Elizabeth Mason and John Bushel, June 26, 1748.

M. Nehemiah Rodham Mason and Sarah Dade, February 12, 1762.

B. John Blackston, son of N.R.B. Mason, March 10, 1769.

M. George Mason and Elizabeth Hooe, April 22, 1784.

M. William Mason and Anne Stuart, July 11, 1793.

B. Anne, daughter of Dade and Elizabeth Massey, March 19, 1719/20.

D. Benjamin Massey, June 24, 1725.

M. Elizabeth Massey and Henry Dade, July 7, 1726.

M. Elizabeth Massey and James Raddish, August 19, 1726.

M.   Robert Massey and Winifred McCarty, December 20, 1728.

B.   Betty, daughter of Robert and Winifred Massey, September 8, 1731.

M.   Dade Massey and Parthenia Alexander, January 17, 1731/2.

B.   Lee, son of Dade and Parthenia Massey, September 19, 1732.

B.   Robert, son of Robert and Winifred Massey, September 10, 1733.

B.   Dade, son of Dade and Parthenia Massey, October 10, 1734.

D.   Dade Massey, Junior, February 7, 1734/5.

D.   Captain Dade Massey, April 16, 1735.

B.   Winifred, daughter of Robert and Winifred Massey, September 6, 1735.

M.   Parthenia Massey and Townshend Dade, Junior, May 6, 1736.

M.   John Massey and Elizabeth Powel, June 12, 1736.

M.   Anne Massey and Francis Wright, December 7, 1737.

B.   Anne, daughter of Robert and Winifred Massey, August 6, 1738.

B.   Frances, daughter of Robert and Winifred Massey, September 22, 1740.

M.   Sigismond Massey and Mary Stuart, April 4, 1743.

B.   Jane, daughter of Sigismond and Mary Massey, February 8, 1743/4.

B.   Dade, son of Thomas and Helenor Massey, March 2, 1745/6.

B.   Sallie, daughter of Benjamin and Elizabeth Massey, March 8, 1745/6.

D.   Sigismund Massey, June 16, 1746.

B.   Sigismunda Mary, daughter of Sigismund and Mary Massey, June 29, 1746.

B.   Dade, son of Benjamin and Elizabeth Massey, January 6, 1747/8.

B.   Taliaferro, son of Benjamin and Elizabeth Massey, April 22, 1749.

M.   Betty Massey and John Washington, November 17, 1749.

B.   Frances, daughter of Benjamin and Elizabeth Massey, July 10, 1751.

B.   Thomas, son of Thomas and Elizabeth Massey, June 1, 1752.

M.   Behethland Massey and Thomas Bunbury, August 30, 1752.

M.   Mary Massey and Horatio Dade, January 14, 1753.

B.   Robert, son of Thomas and Eleanor Massey, November 16, 1757.

B.   Anne, daughter of Charles and Martha Massey, January 21, 1758.

B.   Mary, daughter of Thomas and Mary Massey, April 15, 1760.

M.   Jane Massey and John Waugh, April 22, 1761.

M.   Winifred Massey and Elisha Powel, December 20, 1761.

B.   John, son of Thomas and Eleanor Massey, September 20, 1762.

B.   Martha, daughter of Charles and Martha Massey, September 22, 1762.

B.   Eleanor, daughter of Thomas and Eleanor Massey, March 24, 1765.

M.   Sigismunda Mary Massey and William Alexander, April 18, 1765.

B.   Winifred, daughter of Charles and Martha Massey, December 4, 1765.

M.   Elizabeth Massey and [blank] Coad, December [blank], 1766.

M.   Sigismund Massey and Sarah Short, July 16, 1772.

M.   William Massey and Hannah Settle, February 8, 1784.

M.   Ann Massey and John Perry, May 26, 1785.

M.   Eleanor Massey and Huse Mastin, June 1, 1786.

M.   Lovell Massey and Sarah Whiting, December 28, 1786.

M.   Eleanor Massey and John Washington, December 24, 1787.

M.   Elizabeth Massey and James Grant, January 10, 1793.

M.   Hellenor Mastin and Thomas Prestridge, December 29, 1726.

M.   Huse Mastin and Eleanor Massey, June 1, 1786.

M.   Grisel Matthew and [mutilated] ho.^{s} McCarty, December 23, 1728.

M.   Patrick Matthews of Nanjemey Parish and Elizabeth Evans of this Parish, August 17, 1725.

M.   John Matthews and Anne Bussey, July 21, 1754.

B.   Daniel, son of John and Elizabeth Matthews, April 4, 1755.

B. Elizabeth and Sarah, daughters of John and Elizabeth Matthews, April 2, 1757.

B. Mary, daughter of John and Elizabeth Matthews, January 28, 1760.

B. Mildred, daughter of John and Anne Matthews, June 23, 1761.

B. John, son of John and Elizabeth Matthews, May 5, 1768.

M. Mary Matthews and Andrew Grant, April 26, 1770.

M. William Matthews and Ann Mary Grant, December 5, 1781.

M. Henry Duval Maugeur and Leila Drummond, April 30, 1758.

B. Henry Duval, son of Henry Duval and Lalia Maujeur, January 31, 1759.

D. Sarah Mealy, September 27, 1718.

D. Elizabeth Mealy, June 29, 1725.

B. Mary, daughter of Daniel and Margaret Mealy, [mutilated; circa 1724].

M. Elizabeth Mealy and Thomas Lewis, October 5, 1730.

D. Margaret, wife of Daniel Mealy, December 15, 1738.

D. Daniel Mealy, March 14, 1742/3.

D. John Mease, April 10, 1733.

D. Mary Mease, April 23, 1747.

MEHONY : MEHONEY : MEHORNER : MEHORNEY   SEE: MAHONEY &C: Page 89

MENNIS   SEE: MINNIS, Page 96

M. Mary Mercer and Daniel McCarty, April 3, 1764.

M. Elizabeth Miflin and James Cope of Hanover Parish, December 17, 1746.

M. Elizabeth Miller and Jacob Williams, December 3, 1747.

M. Thomas Mills and Mary Bussey, January 2, 1748/9.

M. Francis Mills and Margaret Handlee, April 6, 1751.

B. Lizzy, daughter of Francis and Margaret Mills, March 19, 1752.

M. Margaret Mills and Henry Davis, November 5, 1758.

M. Hannah Mills and James Brown, January 31, 1786.

M. Callohill Minnis and Elizabeth Holmon, November 16, 1740.

B. Frances, daughter of Collohill and Elizabeth Mennis, September 23, 1741.

B. Mary, daughter of Callahill and Elizabeth Minnis, October 5, 1743.

B. Charles, son of Collochan and Elizabeth Minnis, January 21, 1745/6.

B. Calawell, son of Calawell and Elizabeth Minnis, May 15, 1751.

B. Francis, son of Eleanor Minnis, February 20, 1759.

M. John Minor of Brunswick Parish and Margaret Sumner of Overwharton
    Parish, February 3, 1740/1.

M. Jane Minor and William Kelly, March 30, 1758.

M. Henry Mintoe of Overwharton Parish and Lurina Ward of this Parish,
    January 16, 1737/8.

M. Priscilla Mirax and Joshua Sebastian, March 10, 1748/9.

M. Anthony Mislin and Elizabeth Day of Strother's Parish, May 5, 1735.

M. William Mitchel and Behethland Johnston, September 4, 1787.

M. Elizabeth Mizing and Richard Harmon, March 28, 1746.

D. Mary, daughter of George and Jane Monk, August 8, 1716.

D. Sarah, daughter of George and Jane Monk, September 24, 1716.

M. William Monroe and Jemima Smith of Washington Parish, April 2, 1746.

M. Andrew Monroe and Margaret Washington, December 21, 1761.

M. Mary Monroe and Price Thomas, November 7, 1779.

M. Ann Monroe and Jeremiah Kirk, August 18, 1785.

M. James Monteith and Leah Owens, August 23, 1763.

M. Richard Moody and Elizabeth Townly, February 5, 1758.

B. John, son of Richard and Elizabeth Moody, January 19, 1759.

B. Margaret, daughter of Richard and Elizabeth Moody, February 14, 1761.

M. Anne Moody and William Purchase, July 3, 1775.

M. Elizabeth More and Leonard Martin, December 28, 1764.

D. John Morgan, February 10, 1730/1.

M. Edward Moring and Catherine Greenleves, October 16, 1779.

M. Patrick Morrow and Mary Delaunder, October 6, 1716.

B. James Morton, March 21, 1733/4.

D. Mary, daughter of John Moss, August 15, 1716.

D. Catherine Moss, April 1, 1717.

B. William, son of William and Margaret Moss, March 10, 1717/8.

B. Jane, daughter of John and Elizabeth Moss, April 7, 1718.

B. Jane, daughter of Thomas Moss, deceased, and Mary, his wife, November 16, 1719.

D. Sarah, daughter of John Moss, May 1, 1720.

D. Robert, son of John Moss, May 18, 1720.

D. Jane, daughter of Mary Moss, November 14, 1720.

B. Sarah, daughter of John and Elizabeth Moss, September 17, 1722.

M. Jane Moss and John Kelly, December 21, 1722.

D. John Moss, August 20, 1723.

B. William Moss's child, December 30, 1723.

M. John Moss and Mary Ross, April 27, 1724.

M. Mary Moss and John Taylor, August 19, 1724.

D. Elizabeth, daughter of Thomas and Mary Moss, October 22, 1724.

B. Rae, son of John and Mary Moss, June 27, 1725.

B. Jesse, son of William and Margaret Moss, March 3, 1725/6.

B. Jean, daughter of John and Mary Moss, June 14, 1727.

D. Jean, daughter of John and Mary Moss, June 15, 1727.

M. Sylvester Moss and Frances Kelly, July 7, 1727.

B.   Margaret, daughter of John and Margaret Moss, August 1, 1727.

D.   Frances Moss, June 4, 1729.

B.   Elizabeth, daughter of William and Margaret Moss, April 10, 1731.

B.   Thomas, son of William and Margaret Moss, October 3, 1733.

M.   Silvester Moss and Elizabeth Reid, August 25, 1735.

D.   John Moss, November 1, 1735.

B.   Francis, son of William and Margaret Moss, January 30, 1735/6.

M.   Mary Moss and Nicholas Savin, May 5, 1736.

B.   Anne, daughter of Silvester and Elizabeth Moss, October 1, 1736.

B.   Elizabeth, daughter of Silvester and Anne Moss, December 15, 1737.

B.   Margaret, daughter of William and Margaret Moss, November 15, 1738.

B.   Moses, son of Silvester and Elizabeth Moss, February 13, 1738/9.

M.   Alce Moss and Richard Sebastian, June 1, 1742.

B.   Peggy, daughter of William and Elizabeth Moss, February 16, 1743/4.

M.   Helenor Moss and John Jones, August 16, 1744.

B.   William, son of William and Elizabeth Moss, May 17, 1746.

D.   William Moss, February 13, 1745/6.

B.   John, son of William and Elizabeth Moss, June 9, 1751.

B.   Elizabeth, daughter of William and Elizabeth Moss, December 22, 1753.

M.   Jane Moss and Benjamin Rogers, January 27, 1761.

M.   Thomas Moss and Mary Atwell, September 10, 1772.

M.   Alvin Moxley and Anne Hooe, November 5, 1772.

B.   Anne Dent, daughter of Alvin and Anne Moxley, August 31, 1773.

M.   Peggy Munda and Robert Clift, January 6, 1793. [King George County Mar-
     riage Register records a license issued to Robert Clift and Peggy Minor,
     January 5, 1793].

B.   Grace, daughter of John and Jane Murphy, April 24, 1716.

MURPHY : MURPHEY : MURPHEE : MURPHEW : MORPHEU : MURPHES

B. Grace, daughter of John and Jane Murphy, April 24, 1716

D. Jane, wife of John Murfy, January 6, 1717/8.

M. Helen Morphew and Thomas Williams, September 4, 1723.

D. John Murphy, January 30, 1723/4.

M. Alexander Murphes and Anne Darbin, April 8, 1724.

B. Frances, daughter of Alexander and Anne Murphy, February 24, 1725/6.

B. Sarah, daughter of Alexander and Anne Murphew, October 24, 1731.

B. John, son of John and Margaret Murphee, July 2, 1749.

M. William Lewis Murphey and Elizabeth Smith, April 5, 1768.

M. John Murray and Mary Todd, December 12, 1727

M. Elizabeth Musten and John Gordon, November 24, 1747.

M. Thomas Mustin and Anne Martin, January 19, 1759.

B. William, son of Thomas and Ann Mustin, April 5, 1760.

B. John, son of Thomas and Anne Mustin, August 3, 1761.

B. Sarah, daughter of Thomas and Anne Mustin, May 3, 1763.

B. Margaret, daughter of Thomas and Anne Mustin, January 5, 1766.

B. Thomas, son of Thomas and Anne Mustin, October 17, 1767.

B. Leonard, son of Thomas and Anne Mustin, February 1, 1772.

B. James, son of Thomas and Anne Mustin, February 3, 1774.

N

B. Susanna, daughter of Robert and Ester Nash, August 2, 1746.

M. George Nash and Anne White, January 20, 1769.

B. Mary, daughter of Katherine Naughton*, March 6, 1739/40.

---

* This surname has been altered contemporaneously to Roan. [See Page 114]

B. Katherine Naughton, September 3, 1743.

M. Elizabeth Naylor of Brunswick Parish and John Simpson of Overwharton Parish, August 6, 1735.

D. George Neagle, a servant of George Monk, October 17, 1718.

M. Mary Neal and Benjamin Derrick, September 30, 1729.

M. Sarah Neal and Joshua Lawyer, June 24, 1732.

M. Elizabeth Netherington and William Walker, November 23, 1731.

M. David Nevens and Janet Patterson, June 6, 1759.

B. Mary, daughter of David and Janet Nevens, June 3, 1764.

B. Janet, daughter of David and Janet Nevens, August 27, 1765.

M. David Nevens and Mary Oard, June 28, 1767.

M. Zachariah Newble and Anne Hamit, November 6, 1779.

M. James Newman and Sarah Griffin, December 25, 1759.

M. Elizabeth Newport and Simon Bowling, June 5, 1728.

D. Mary Newton, March 25, 1716.

M. Benjamin Newton and Elizabeth Nicholson, May 6, 1716.

M. Anne Newton and Simon Bowline, December 5, 1722

M. Elizabeth Newton and Thomas Stribling, December 7, 1725.

M. Sarah Newton and William Higgins, December 9, 1732.

M. Benjamin Newton of Hamilton Parish and Jane Colclough of this Parish, October 22, 1740.

M. Elizabeth Nicholson and Benjamin Newton, May 6, 1716.

D. Mary Nicholson, May 13, 1722.

M. Thomas Norfolk and Mary Burket, December 6, 1737.

B. John, son of Thomas and Mary Norfolk, January 4, 1740/1.

M. Thomas Norman and Elizabeth Duncum, February 21, 1736/7.

M. Anne Norman and Jesse Briant, January 1, 1790.

M. John Norris and Sarah Turner, August 29, 1751.

B. William, son of Peter and Anne Noshard*, May 15, 1758.

M. Margaret Noting and Benjamin Mehorner, April 5, 1778.

D. Thomas Nowland, a servant boy of Daniel Mealy, July 29, 1718.

M. Peter Nugent and Martha Sill, both of Hanover Parish, February 15, 1731/2.

O

M. John Oakly and Anne Gordon, February 14, 1744/5.

M. Mary Oard and David Nivens, June 28, 1767.

D. John Oliver, March 5, 1715/6.

B. John, son of John and Margaret Oliver, February 15, 1720/1.

B. Elias, son of John and Margaret Oliver, February 19, 1723/4.

D. Nathaniel and John Oliver, children, suddenly, November 20, 1725.

D. Sarah Oliver, January 30, 1725/6.

B. George, son of John and Margaret Oliver, January 29, 1726/7.

B. George, son of John and Elizabeth Oliver, January 15, 1727/8.

B. Margaret, daughter of John and Margaret Oliver, January 3, 1732/3.

B. John, son of John and Margaret Oliver, October 18, 1735.

B. Mary, daughter of John and Margaret Oliver, April 7, 1738.

D. Mary, daughter of John and Margaret Oliver, May 28, 1740.

B. Rebecca, daughter of John and Margaret Oliver, September 29, 1741.

M. George Oliver and Jemima Regan, August 1, 1745.

M. Margaret Oliver and Nathaniel Hogdon, March 2, 1746/7.

M. Rebecca Oliver and William Mahony, September 15, 1759.

B. John, son of John and Mildred Olver, July 14, 1760.

* This surname may be Hushard

B.   Elisha, daughter of John and Winifred Oliver, April 26, 1768.

B.   Sarah, daughter of John and Mildred Oliver, October 1, 1772.

M.   Nancy Oliver and James Giles [or Gibs], March 24, 1788.

M.   Mary Oneal and John Alias, September 17, 1722.

D.   Mary Oneal, November 12, 1730.

B.   William, son of Mary Ore, September 2, 1760.

M.   Elinor Ormond and John Conah, June 13, 1725.

M.   Mary Orr and David Cable, September 7, 1766.

D.   Thomas Osburn, October 18, 1728.

OVERALL   :   OVERHALL

B.   Frances, daughter of William and Mary Overall, August 22, 1716.

D.   Jane Overall, mother of William Overall, April 5, 1718.

M.   John Overhall and Mary Ellis, October 8, 1722.

D.   William Overall, January 17, 1725/6.

B.   Sarah, daughter of John and Mary Overall, February 7, 1725/6.

M.   Mary Overall and Anthony Kitchen, August 31, 1727.

M.   Sarah Overhall and John Dagg, November 14, 1729.

B.   Mary, daughter of John and Mary Overhall, March 19, 1730/1.

M.   Elizabeth Overhall of this Parish and John Whitledge of Hamilton Parish, September 15, 1733.

M.   Frances Overhall of this Parish and Nathaniel Whitledge of Hamilton Parish, October 27, 1733.

M.   Sarah Overhall and Joseph Powel, September 21, 1750.

M.   Mary Overhall and James Bowling, February 11, 1750/1.

M.   Behethland Overhall and James Cunningham, June 21, 1757.

B.   John, son of Susanna Owens, February 13, 1745/6.

M.   Susanna Owens and Thomas Timons, May 14, 1749.

M. Leah Owens and James Monteith, August 23, 1763.

B. Essena, daughter of Aaron Owens, November 30, 1767.

B. William, son of John and Dulcibella Owens, September 11, 1768.

M. Lucinda Owens and Thomas Jett, January 12, 1775.

M. Jane Owens and James Staples, February 12, 1778.

M. Aaron Owens and Catherine Wilson, March 26, 1785.

M. Aaron Owens and Amie Mannard, May 13, 1791.

M. Letty Owens and Eli Mehorney, June 23, 1792.

M. Elizabeth Oxford and Richard Thomson, June 3, 1724.

M. Elizabeth Oxford and Samuel Bowline, October 8, 1731.

B. John, son of Samuel and Mary Oxford, November 3, 1731.

B. Anne, daughter of Samuel and Mary Oxford, December 28, 1733.

B. Elizabeth, daughter of Samuel and Mary Oxford, August 7, 1736.

M. Edward Oxives and Elinor Dunfee, November 27, 1724.

P

B. Isobell, daughter of John and Mary Palmer, September 12, 1740.

M. Thomas Paremane and Mary Lacy, August 28, 1751.

M. James Park and Sally Dade, March 4, 1796. [King George County Marriage
    Register notes license issued to James Parke and Sarah Dade].

M. Thomas Lewis Parrat and Hester Stribling, April 16, 1744.

D. John Parsons, December 9, 1732.

M. David Parsons and Elizabeth Jones, February 25, 1759.

M. Janet Patterson and David Nevens, June 6, 1759.

M. John Patton and Martha Payn of Hanover Parish, April 3, 1746.

M. John Pavier and Anne Ambrie, June 1, 1738.

PAYNE : PAYN : PAIN : PANE

D. Richard Pain, April 21, 1721.

D. William Payn, January 14, 1731/2.

M. Sarah Payn and John Lacky, June 6, 1737.

M. Martha Payn of Hanover Parish and John Patton, April 3, 1746.

M. Jeremiah Payne and Judith Duke, May 25, 1760.

B. Mary, daughter of William Payne, September 8, 1764.

B. Sarah, daughter of Susanna Pane, August 7, 1765.

B. Rice, son of Virgin Pain, August 28, 1766.

B. Frank, son of Francis and Anne Payne, December 1, 1766.

B. Elias, son of Susanna Payne, March 10, 1767.

B. John, son of William and Elizabeth Payne, April 15, 1769.

B. John, son of Virgin Pane, October 13, 1772.

M. Anne Peach and Solomon Hardwick, September 25, 1748.

M. Frances Peak and Benjamin Clift, February 16, 1772.

B. Mary Anne, daughter of William Peake, February 12, 1757.

M. Susanna Pearson and John Alexander, December 15, 1734.

M. Elizabeth Peck and Thomas Stribling, March 8, 1752.

M. William Peck and Jane Curry, August 3, 1766.

B. Sarah, daughter of William and Jane Peck, August 28, 1767.

B. Stribling, son of William and Jane Peck, September 27, 1768.

B. Mildred, daughter of William and Jane Peck, May 21, 1771.

B. Robert, son of William and Jane Peck, June 14, 1772.

B. David, son of William and Jane Peck, April 11, 1773.

B. John, son of Reuben and Eleanor Peck, December 3, 1773.

PEED : PEDE : PEDES

B. Francis, son of James and Anne Pedes, January 15, 1738/9.

B. Philip, son of James and Anne Peed, October 3, 1740.

M. John Peed and Behethland Jones, February 14, 1770.

B. Mildred, daughter of John and Behethland Peed, September 22, 1772.

M. Joanna Pede and Rush Marshall, November 23, 1779.

M. Dolly Peed and John White, January 3, 1790.

M. Elizabeth Pennal and Thomas Vincent, April 3, 1749.

D. Robert Pennuell, husband of Thomasin Pennuell, March 20, 1717/8.

B. James, son of James and Alce Penny, February 2, 1732/3.

B. Sarah, daughter of James and [blank] Penny, January 10, 1734/5.

PERRY : PARRY : [! GARRY !]

B. William, son of Simon and Martha Perry, May 2, 1744.

B. Susanna, daughter of Simon and Martha Garry, September 10, 1749.

B. Elisha, son of Simon and Martha Parry, February 26, 1752.

B. Simon, son of Simon and Martha Perry, January 12, 1756.

M. Elisha Perry and Gracey Waugh, January 30, 1783.

M. Simon Perry and Anne Hartly, December 25, 1783.

M. John Perry and Ann Massey, May 26, 1785.

M. Simon Perry and Elizabeth Fountain, February 16, 1791.

PESTRIDGE : SEE: PRESTRIDGE AND DUNCOMB

M. Francis Peyton and Frances Dade, April 24, 1755.

M. Henry Peyton and Susanna Fowke, March 15, 1764.

M. Carnaby Peyton and Mary Hilton, July 5, 1764.

M. Mary Pew and Ephraim Simmons, April 13, 1740.

M. John Philips and Mary Edwards, February 27, 1737/8.

M. Thomas Philips and Priscilla Bolling, April 13, 1760.

M. Thomas Philips and Isabel Holland, June 14, 1772.

M. Charles Philips and Dully Carver, August 19, 1787.

M. Elizabeth Philips and James Grisset, May 19, 1791.

B. John, son of William and Elizabeth Pickett, February 26, 1734/5.

B. Martine, son of William and Elizabeth Pickett, December 25, 1736.

PILCHER : PILSHER

B. William, son of Stephen and Jane Pilcher, March 3, 1715/6.

D. John Pilsher, January 16, 1735/6.

M. Jane Pilsher and David Bowline, September 10, 1741.

M. Judith Pilcher of Hanover Parish and John Campbell, August 20, 1746.

M. John Pimm and Ruth Finchum, December 29, 1760.

M. Elizabeth Plunkett of Hanover Parish and John Willis, January 17, 1734/5.

POATES : POTES : POTTS

B. Richard, son of William and Honor Poates, [mutilated]   1724.

D. William Potes, February 21, 1733/4.

M. Honour Poates and James Rea, July 2, 1738.

B. Sarah, daughter of Richard and Elizabeth Potes, December 21, 1771.

D. Lancelot Pockley, September 24, 1736.

M. Lucinda Pollard and William Bruce, December 20, 1787.

M. Anne Poplar and Morice Cunningham, April 2, 1738.

B. Anne, daughter of Thomas and Anne Porter, October 13, 1717.

M. Mary Porter and William Toul, October 15, 1722.

Baptized Benjamin, son of Thomas and Anne Porter, May 1, 1725.

B. Joseph, son of Thomas and Anne Porter, August 7, 1727.

D. Anne Porter, September 22, 1727.

B. Anne, daughter of Thomas and Anne Porter, March 15, 1731/2.

B. John, son of Thomas and Anne Porter, August 4, 1734.

M. Parthenia Posey and Rawleigh Rye, May 7, 1790. [The King George County Marriage Register records a license for Rolly Rye and Parthenia Posey].

POTES : SEE: POATES : POTES : POTTS

M. Susanna Potter and Daniel Fitzhugh, October 24, 1772.

POWEL : POWELL

D. William, son of William and Amy Powell, October 30, 1716.

B. Elizabeth, daughter of William and Amy Powell, November 17, 1717.

D. Joseph Powell, brother of William Powell, December 19, 1717.

B. John, son of William and Amy Powell, August 16, 1720.

M. Jane Powell and Elijah Wood, June 30, 1722.

M. Grace Powel and James Berry, May 28, 1723.

B. Jean, daughter of William and Amy Powell, June 20, 1725.

D. Richard Powel, January 15, 1725/6.

D. Elizabeth, daughter of William and Amy Powell, September 27, 1728.

M. Jemima Powell and Edward Derrick, January 2, 1728/9.

M. Frances Powel and John Johnson, November 18, 1731.

B. Richard, son of William and Amia Powel, June 1, 1733.

D. Grace Powel, October 29, 1734.

M. Elizabeth Powel and John Massey, June 12, 1736.

B. Amia, daughter of William and Amia Powell, September 10, 1736.

M. Katherine Powel and Benjamin Derrick, July 29, 1737.

B. Elisha, son of William and Amy Powel, May 2, 1739.

D. John, son of William and Amy Powell, November 27, 1739.

D. Jane, daughter of William and Amy Powell, January 28, 1730/40.

108

D. Richard, son of William and Amy Powell, December 27, 1742.

D. William Powell, January 20, 1745/6.

M. William Powell and Elizabeth Regan, April 2, 1747.

M. Joseph Powel and Sarah Overhall, September 21, 1750.

B. Elizabeth, daughter of Joseph and Mary Powell, December 13, 1751.

M. Amy Powel and Anthony Buckner Thomas, April 20, 1755.

B. Jane, daughter of Joseph and Sarah Powel, December 15, 1753.

B. William, son of Joseph and Sarah Powell, May 5, 1756.

B. John, son of Joseph and Sarah Powell, December 28, 1758.

M. Elisha Powel and Winifred Massey, December 20, 1761.

M. James Power and Mary Lewis, October 19, 1724.

D. Elizabeth Power, June 27, 1725.

M. Elizabeth Powers of Caroline County and James Gouch, February 21, 1762.

D. John Pratt, February 12, 1737/8.

B. Susanna, daughter of Thomas and Margaret Pratt, February 8, 1756.

B. Molly, daughter of Thomas and Margaret Pratt, January 28, 1758.

B. John Burkett, son of Thomas Pratt, August 6, 1761.

B. Thomas, son of Thomas and Margaret Pratt, June 28, 1765.

M. Margaret Pratt and Bernard Hooe, November 2, 1771.

M. Mildred Pratt and Henry Washington, March 12, 1779.

M. Susanna Pratt and William Hooe, November 13, 1782.

M. Thomas Pratt and Jane Brockenbrough, June 23, 1785.

PRESTRIDGE : PESTRIDGE

D. [Torn] mison Pestridge, November 1, 1725.

B. Alse, daughter of Thomas and Anne Prestridge, October 12, 1726.

M. Thomas Prestridge and Helleanor Mastin, December 29, 1726.

B. [Torn] Prestridge, February 3, 1729/30.

D. Thomas Prestridge, March 22, 1731/2.

B. Thomas, son of Thomas and Anne Prestridge, February 28, 1732/3.

B. Elizabeth, daughter of Thomas and Anne Prestridge, March 4, 1734/5.

D. Thomas Prestridge, April 9, 1737.

M. Anne Prestridge and William Steel, April 27, 1742.

B. John, son of Benjamin Duncomb by Sarah Pestridge, December 28, 1748.

B. William, son of Sarah Pestridge, February 11, 1750/1.

B. Linny, daughter of Thomas and Sarah Pestridge, December 16, 1756.

M. Sarah Pestridge and Reuben Bates, December 4, 1757.

M. Michael Price and Anne Dennis, August 24, 1727.

M. Mary Price and Massey Thomas, November 28, 1731.

M. Thomas Price and Sarah Buckner, December 31, 1734.

B. Anne, daughter of Thomas and Sarah Price, December 20, 1735.

B. Anthony, son of Thomas and Sarah Price, November 12, 1736.

B. Margaret, daughter of Thomas and Sarah Price, February 10, 1737/8.

B. Merryday, son of Thomas and Sarah Price, September 5, 1739.

B. Elizabeth, daughter of Thomas and Sarah Price, June 3, 1741.

B. Sarah, daughter of Thomas and Sarah Price, May 13, 1743.

B. Katherine, daughter of Thomas and Sarah Price, February 7, 1744/5.

M. Nathaniel Price and Jane Blinkenship, July 25, 1746.

B. Susanna, daughter of Thomas and Sarah Price, March 20, 1746/7.

B. John, son of Thomas and Sarah Grice*, June 5, 1749.

B. Mary, daughter of William and Sarah Price, January 1, 1754.

---

*   This is one of the several obvious errors in these recordings - Grice
    for Price and note Garry for Perry [Parry].

M. Elizabeth Price and Moses Burgess, May 30, 1762.

M. [Blank] Price and Edward Burgess, February 20, 1765.

M. Anthony Price and Elizabeth Stribling, January 17, 1768.

B. Sarah, daughter of Anthony and Elizabeth Price, July 27, 1769.

B. Thomas, son of Anthony and Elizabeth Price, March 31, 1772.

B. Buckner, son of Anthony and Elizabeth Price, September 21, 1774.

M. Molly Price and James Williams, April 24, 1782.

M. John Price and Susanna Jones, May 5, 1786. [King George County Marriage
    Register shows license issued to John Price, Junior, and Susanna Jones].

M. Sally Price and Benjamin Roach, December 22, 1786.

M. Mary Price and Moses Mardus, February 27, 1791.

D. Anthony Prorser, March 5, 1732/3.

D. Frances Proser, September 4, 1732.

M. Pemberton Proudlove and Alse Ware, February 10, 1717/8.

D. Pemberton Proudlove, October 22, 1725.

M. Alice Proudlove and Christopher Bell, June 4, 1726.

M. Peter Puckett and Amie Keith, December 27, 1775.

M. William Purchase and Anne Moody, July 3, 1775.

M. Elizabeth Purtle and Joseph Crismand, February 16, 1752.

                                Q

M. William Quarles and Lucy Alexander, October 20, 1784.

                                R

RADDISH : SEE: REDDISH

B. Anne, daughter of Edward and Briget Raddy, May 27, 1743.

M. Sarah Radford and Michael Black, December 3, 1752.

RAGAN : SEE: REAGAN : REGAN

D. Matthew Ragan, March 30, 1716.

RALLINS : RALLINGS :   SEE: RAWLINS : RAWLINGS   &c.

M. Anne Ramsay and Richard Dixon, April 13, 1775.

M. Nicholas Randolph and Margaret Raddish, February 21, 1733/4.

D. Thomas Randolph, December 16, 1735.

M. William Randolph and Mary Grymes, May 18, 1770.

M. Robert Rankins and Jane Fingleson, December 26, 1756.

M. Mary Rankins and Henry Ward, June 14, 1775.

D. James Ranton, July 25, 1717.

M. Frances Rawlett and William Staples, February 18, 1790.

RAWLINS : RAWLINGS : RALLINS : RALLINGS

M. Judith Rawlins and Thomas Lacy, November 9, 1716.

M. Mary Rallings and William Baxter, April 1, 1735.

B. John, son of Thomas and Mary Rawlens, March 13, 1742/3.

B. Joseph, son of Thomas and Mary Rawlins, February 15, 1744/5.

M. Richard Rawlings and Katherine Rice of Washington Parish, April 11, 1746.

M. Rebecca Rallings and Archibald Campbell, January 15, 1753.

M. James Rallings and Margaret Stribling, January 5, 1778.

M. Joseph Rallins and Elizabeth Mardus, May 25, 1778.

M. Sarah Rallings and Thomas Guteridge, May 16, 1782.

M. Margaret Rallins and William Hudson, March 10, 1785.

RAYMOND : RYMOND

M. John Raymond and Katherine Campbell, January 12, 1735/6.

B. Richard, son of John and Katherine Rymond, October 20, 1736.

112

B. John, son of John and Katherine Raymond, December 7, 1738.

B. Mary, daughter of John and Katherine Raymond, November 15, 1740.

D. Katherine, wife of John Raymond, January 8, 1743/4.

M. John Raymond and Margaret Robertson, February 27, 1746/ 7.

D. Mary, wife of James Rea, November 6, 1737.

M. James Rea and Honour Poates, July 2, 1738.

D. James Rea, September 4, 1740.

REDDISH : RADDISH

B. Mary, daughter of James and Elizabeth Reddish, May 5, 1721.

M. Sarah Raddish and John Gordon, January 24, 1722/3.

M. Katherine Raddish and William Vaint, August 27, 1723.

M. James Raddish and Elizabeth Massey, August 19, 1726.

M. Robert Raddish and Helen Durham, November 10, 1727.

B. Mary, daughter of Robert and Helenor Raddish, February 28, 1731/2.

M. Margaret Raddish and Nicholas Randolph, February 21, 1733/4.

B. John, son of Robert Raddish, August 20, 1734.

M. Robert Raddish and Jane Allerton, October 12, 1735.

B. Joel, son of Joseph and Sarah Raddish, February 22, 1747/8.

B. Winifred, daughter of Joseph and Sarah Reddish, August 26, 1749.

B. Behethland, daughter of Joseph and Sarah Reddish, August 20, 1751.

B. Sadyris, daughter of Joseph and Sarah Raddish, March 21, 1754.

B. Eleanor, daughter of Joseph and Sarah Raddish, March 30, 1759.

M. Bartholomew Redman and Jean Elkin, June 24, 1727.

REGAN : REAGAN   SEE: RIGGIN : RIGGINS : ROGAN

B. Elizabeth, daughter of Charles and Elizabeth Riggin, October 20, 1731.

B. Katherine, daughter of Charles and Elizabeth Reagan, July 25, 1733.

B. Katherine, daughter of Charles and Elizabeth Regan, February 1, 1734/5.

B. John, son of Charles and Elizabeth Regan, August 23, 1736.

B. James, son of Charles and Elizabeth Regan, April 9, 1738.

B. Elisha, son of Charles and Elizabeth Regan, April 19, 1740.

B. Winifred, daughter of Bridget Regan, May 16, 1744.

D. William Regan, November 21, 1744.

M. Jemima Regan and George Oliver, August 1, 1745.

B.. Isaac, son of Margaret Regan, December 22, 1746.

M. Elizabeth Regan and William Powell, April 2, 1747.

M. Margaret Regan and Jacob Johnson, October 13, 1748.

M. Charles Regg and Sarah Day of Hanover Parish, July 17, 1746.

M. Elizabeth Reid and Silvester Moss, August 25, 1735.

B. John, son of Thomas and Elizabeth Reilly, September 17, 1716.

B. Phillis, daughter of Thomas and Elizabeth Reilly, November 14, 1717.

B. Anne, daughter of Thomas and Elizabeth Reilly, January 19, 1720/1.

REINEY : REANEY

B. John, son of Jane Reaney, March 7, 1748/9.

M. Jane Reiney and William Jones, April 20, 1752.

M. Margaret Reins and James Stuart, March 24, 1724/5.

M. Thomas Relins and Mary Rigby, July 16, 1742.

M. Mary Rian and John Christy, May 4, 1749.

B. John, son of Hugh and Mary Rice, July 26, 1716.

M. Katherine Rice of Washington Parish and Richard Rawlings, April 11, 1746.

M. Frances Richards and Horatio Dade, October 5, 1749.

M. William Richardson and Clary Mannard, January 16, 1791. [King George
    County Marriage Register gives the name of the bride as Clary Manning].

B. Mary Anne, daughter of Alexander and Anne Rigby, December 2, 1720.

B. Elizabeth, daughter of Alexander and Anne Rigby, April 10, 1722.

B. Sarah, daughter of Alexander and Anne Rigby, March 10, 1727/8.

M. Alexander Rigby and Jane Johnson, December 28, 1729.

M. Mary Rigby and Thomas Relins, July 16, 1742.

    RIGGIN : RIGGINS : ROGAN   SEE: REGAN : REAGAN

D. Elizabeth, daughter of William and Elizabeth Bridget Riggin, October 7,
    1717.

B. John, son of William and Elizabeth Bridget Riggins, November 3, 1717.

D. John, son of William and Elizabeth Bridget Riggins, September 12, 1718.

B. Powel, son of William and Elizabeth Bridget Riggins, April 10, 1722.

B. Keziah, daughter of William and Bridget Regan, February 2, 1726/7.

B. Elizabeth, daughter of William and Bridget Rogan, April 20, 1731.

B. Elizabeth, daughter of Charles and Elizabeth Riggin, October 20, 1731.

B. Bridget, daughter of William and Bridget Rogan, June 22, 1733.

D. Bridget Rogan, June 22, 1733.

M. Jane Riggin and Samuel Evans, June 29, 1746.

M. Keziah Riggins and Alexander Douglas, May 21, 1749.

M. Benjamin Roach and Sally Price, December 22, 1786.

B. Mary, daughter of Katherine Naughton*, March 6, 1739/40.

M. Mary Robins and Timothy Barrington, October 15, 1731.

M. Margaret Robertson and John Raymond, February 27, 1746/7.

D. [Torn] Robinson, June 21, 1725.

B. Sarah, daughter of Margaret Robison, December 27, 1725.

B. James, son of Edward and Mary Roddy, January 20, 1744/5.

---

*   This surname has been altered contemporaneously to Roan. [See Page 99]

M. Sarah Roe and John Skinner, September 15, 1743.

   ROGAN   SEE: RIGGIN : RIGGINS   AND   REGAN : REAGAN

   ROGERS : RODGERS

M. Mary Rogers and William Colclough, December 30, 1741.

B. Rice, son of William and Frances Rogers, June 17, 1746.

B. Behethlem, daughter of William and Frances Rodgers, March 13, 1747/8.

M. Joseph Rogers and Anne Burgess, October 24, 1749.

B. Ann, daughter of Grigsby and Grace Rogers, October 11, 1750.

B. Mary, daughter of Grigsby and Mary Rodgers, March 30, 1752.

B. Robert, son of William and Frances Rogers, October 9, 1753.

B. Margaret, daughter of William and Frances Rogers, August 17, 1756.

B. Winifred, daughter of William and Frances Rogers, March 21, 1759.

M. Benjamin Rogers and Jane Moss, January 27, 1761.

M. Behethland Rogers and John Chandler, September 17, 1767.

B. James, son of Benjamin and Jane Rogers, May 10, 1768.

M. Sarah Rogers and Benjamin Clift, December 6, 1772.

M. Margaret Rogers and John Gordon, Junior, November 22, 1776.

M. Anne Rodgers and John Clift, September 29, 1779.

M. Susanna Rogers and Daniel Beattie, August 2, 1781.

M. Hosea Rogers and Caty Clift, January 22, 1783.

M. Anne Rogers and John Curry, December 25, 1783.

M. [Blank] Rogers and [Blank] Wiggins, August 12, 1787.

M. Isaac Rodgers and Clarinda Lewis, December 11, 1791.

M. Susanna Rorh and William Hanson, November 19, 1725.

B. Maxfield, son of William and Mary Rose, November 27, 1717.

M. Pleasant Rose and John Smith, September 30, 1725.

M. John Rose and Lucy Bennet, October 14, 1731.

B. Bennet, son of John and Lucy Rose, January 5, 1731/2.

B. Francis, son of William and Mary Rose, March 2, 1734/5.

M. William Rose and Sarah Day, June 6, 1737.

B. William, son of William and Sarah Rose, December 5, 1737.

M. The Rev. Mr. Robert Rose of St.Anne's Parish and Anne Fitzhugh of this Parish, November 6, 1740.

B. Elizabeth, daughter of William and Sarah Rose, December 28, 1740.

B. Henry, son of the Rev. Mr. Robert Rose of Essex County and Anne, his wife, December 20, 1741.

B. Hugh, son of the Reverend Robert and Anne Rose, September 18, 1743.

B. Mary, daughter of William and Sarah Rose, March 2, 1743/4.

M. Mary Rose and Richard Lee, June 29, 1744.

B. Patrick, son of Reverend Robert and Anne Rose, July 4, 1745.

B. Zacharia, son of William and Sarah Rose, June 2, 1747.

B. Charles, son of Reverend Robert and Anne Rose, August 17, 1747.

B. William, son of Futrel and Anne Rose, March 18, 1747/8.

M. Isaac Rose and Rachel Grigsby, December 19, 1751.

M. Robert Rose and Frances Jones, June 7, 1752.

B. Elizabeth, daughter of Margaret Rose, December 24, 1753.

M. Francis Rose and Hester Stribling, May 31, 1756.

M. Jane Rose and Oswald Chrismund, June 27, 1757.

B. William, son of Francis and Hesther Rose, July 26, 1757.

M. Elias Rose and Sarah Sweney, September 2, 1758.

B. Isaac, son of William and Sarah Rose, March 2, 1759.

B. Isaac, son of William and Sarah Rose, January 20, 1761.

B. Anne, daughter of Francis and Mary Rose, January 4, 1762.

M. Elizabeth Rose and Daniel Lewis, August 31, 1762.

B. William, son of William and Sarah Rose, February 20, 1764.

B. Bennett, son of Francis and Mary Rose, March 18, 1766.

M. Mary Rose and John Carver, July 17, 1768.

B. John, son of Francis and Mary Rose, October 22, 1768.

B. Anne, daughter of Caton and Mary Rose, July 4, 1774.

B. Joel Stribling, son of Francis and Mary Rose, September 29, 1774.

M. John Rose and Anne Swillakeen, January 4, 1776.

M. Zachariah Rose and Sarah Taylor, March 19, 1778.

M. Elias Rose and Mary Brooke, March 30, 1778.

M. Frances Rose and William Crysell, November 17, 1782.

M. Mary Rose and Andrew Thompson, January 2, 1787.

B. Sarah, daughter of Alexander and Elizabeth Ross, July 17, 1717.

D. Elizabeth Ross, October 10, 1718.

D. Hugh Ross, August 20, 1720.

M. Mary Ross and John Moss, April 27, 1724.

B. William, son of Alexander and Sarah Ross, February 8, 1726/7.

D. Alexander Ross, November 14, 1729.

M. Sarah Ross and John Wilkison, November 13, 1730.

D. Mary Ross, January 17, 1735/6.

B. John, son of Jane Ross, January 20, 1742/3.

M. Rachel Rosser of Hanover Parish and John Jackson, January 31, 1731/2.

B. David, son of Hilliare and Elizabeth Roussau, November 2, 1717.

D. Hilliare Roussau, June 30, 1720.

M. Thomas Roy and Susanna Hooe, September 7, 1777.

D. [Blank] Rutland, a child, January 27, 1725/6.

D. John Rutland, January 31, 1725/6.

M. John Russell and Molly Dodd, December 18, 1791.

M. Patrick Ryan and Elizabeth Edwards, May 6, 1723.

M. James Seaton Ryan and Jennet Bennet, April 5, 1763.

M. Rawleigh Rye and Parthenia Posey, May 7, 1790. [King George County Mar-
    riage Register records a license issued for Rolly Rye and Parthenia Posey].

    RYMOND   SEE: RAYMOND

                                    S

    SABASTIAN   SEE: SEBASTIAN

M. Thomas Sachary and Anne Griffin, April 21, 1760.

    SACHEVEREL : SHIVEREL : SHEVRY   SEE: CHIVREL : CHIVERAL

M. Clement Shevry and Mary McIntosh, August 11, 1751.

B. Elijah, son of Clement and Mary Shiverel, in Maryland, August 30, 1757.

B. Elizabeth, daughter of Clement and Mary Sacheverel, December 8, 1759.

B. Jane, daughter of Clement Sacheverel, August 25, 1763.

B. William, son of Clement and Mary Sacheveral, October 28, 1763 [? 1764].

M. Clement Sacheverel and Eleanor Hodge, November 8, 1763.

B. Mary, daughter of Clement and Eleanor Sacheverel, July 29, 1766.

M. William Sacheverel and Elizabeth Trunnel, February 26, 1784.

M. Mary Sacheverel and John Deacon, May 15, 1785.

M. Sarah Sanders of St.Paul's Parish and William Clark of Overwharton
    Parish, August 5, 1752.

M. Samuel Sandys and Barbara Bagg, September 12, 1724.

M. Joseph Sanford and Jane Bunbury, May 8, 1766.

M. Hannah Saunders and Thomas Horton, February 10, 1786.

M. Nicholas Savin and Mary Moss, May 5, 1736.

D. Henry Savine, June 25, 1725.

M. William Scapelan and Anne Holloway, September 29, 1748.

B. Joseph, son of William and Mary Scapelin, October 8, 1757.

M. William Scaplehorn and Mary Stoward, February 21, 1754.

M. Catherine Schofield and George Stone, July 1, 1716.

M. William Scipier and Anne McFarlan, February 17, 1750/1.

M. William Scott and Anne Clifton, February 23, 1727/8.

B. Elizabeth, daughter of William and Anne Scott, February 28, 1727/8.

B. William, son of William and Anne Scott, January 21, 1731/2.

B. Henry, son of William and Anne Scott, May 26, 1734.

B. Alexander, son of William and Anne Scott, April 14, 1736.

B. Jannet, daughter of Doctor William Scott, October 24, 1739.

D. Doctor William Scott, September 17, 1742.

D. Anne, widow of Doctor William Scott, September 11, 1743.

D. John Scott, December 23, 1744.

M. William Scott and Mildred Bunbury, June 18, 1756.

B. John Mildred, son of William and Mildred Scott, October 31, 1757.

M. Alexander Scott and Frances Bunbury, February 22, 1758.

B. Francis, son of Alexander and Frances Scott, June 27, 1759.

M. William Scott and Sarah Gray, April 18, 1765.

B. Anne, daughter of William and Sarah Scott, May 5, 1768.

B. James, son of William and Sarah Scott, September 5, 1771.

B. Jane, daughter of William and Sarah Scott, January 17, 1774.

M. John Mildred Scott and Mary Holland, February 26, 1784.

M. John Scott and Dully Clift, February 15, 1787.

120

SAINT PAUL'S PARISH REGISTER

SCRANAGE : SCRANNAGE   SEE: CRANNIGE : CRANNIDGE

M. James Scribner and Behethland Beach, November 7, 1773.

SCUDAMORE   SEE: SKIDMORE

B. Anne, daughter of William and Elizabeth Scudamore, August 1, 1749.

B. Jane, daughter of James and Frances Seaton, October 29, 1717.

B. George, son of James and Frances Seaton, November 26, 1726.

D. Isaac Seaton, December 10, 1725.

M. Elizabeth Seaton and John Lowry, April 23, 1726.

D. Frances, wife of James Seaton, December 12, 1730.

M. James Seaton and Grace Daunton, March 11, 1730/1.

D. Jane Seaton, January 31, 1735/6.

D. George Seaton, February 21, 1735/6.

B. John, son of James and Grace Seaton, July 16, 1736.

B. George, son of James and Grace Seaton, September 2, 1738.

M. Frances Seaton of this Parish and Warrener Ford of Washington Parish, July 24, 1740.

B. Jane, daughter of James and Grace Seaton, April 17, 1741.

B. William, son of James and Grace Seaton, October 4, 1743.

D. James Seaton, September 20, 1744.

B. John, son of James and Frances Seaton, January 12, 1744/5.

D. Frances, wife of James Seaton, January 26, 1744/5.

M. Grace Seaton and Burdit Clifton, May 18, 1745 .

M. Joseph Sebastian and Anne Martin, February 6, 1717/8.

B. William, son of Joshua and Bethridge Sebastian, January 18, 1720/1.

M. Anne Sebastian and John Allenthrope, April 16, 1723.

B. Anne, daughter of Joseph and Anne Sebastian, February 19, 1724/5.

B. Joshua, son of Joshua and Margaret Sebastian, March 13, 1725/6.

B. Sarah, daughter of William and Elizabeth Sebastian, September 1, 1726.

M. Nicholas Sebastian and Anne Elliott, October 29, 1726.

M. Margaret Sebastian and Robert King, April 26, 1727.

M. Isaac Sebastian and Rachel Spicer, May 11, 1727.

B. Joseph, son of Joseph and Anne Sebastian, February 29, 1727/8.

M. Benjamin Sebastian and Priscilla Elkins, February 16, 1729/30.

B. Rachel, daughter of Isaac and Rachel Sebastian, January 6, 1730/1.

B. Thomas Elliot, son of Nicholas and Anne Sebastian, March 20, 1730/1.

B. Hannah, daughter of Joshua and Margaret Sebastian, July 12, 1731.

B. Thaddeus, son of Joseph and Anne Sebastian, March 9, 1731/2.

D. Thaddeus, son of Joseph and Anne Sebastian, November 24, 1732.

B. Stephen, son of Isaac and Rachel Sebastian, March 3, 1732/3.

B. Anna, daughter of Nicholas and Anne Sebastian, March 2, 1733/4.

B. Elizabeth, daughter of Joseph and Anne Sebastian, March 10, 1733/4.

B. Mary, daughter of Isaac and Rachel Sebastian, April 20, 1734.

D. Elizabeth Sebastian, October 12, 1734.

D. Stephen Sebastian, February 7, 1734/5.

M. Margaret Sebastian and Joseph Sudduth, October 13, 1735.

D. Joshua Sebastian, February 24, 1734/5.

D. Nicholas Sebastian, December 24, 1735.

M. Anne Sebastian and John James, December 29, 1737.

M. Margaret Sebastian and Benjamin Clift, May 6, 1740.

M. Richard Sebastian and Alce Moss, June 1, 1742.

M. Mary Sebastian and William Johnson, January 5, 1743/4.

B. Mary, daughter of Richard and Alice Sebastian, April 30, 1744.

M. Jane Sebastian and David Jamison, May 7, 1744.

M. Rachel Sebastian and James Fletcher, April 21, 1745.

B. Constant, daughter of Richard and Alice Sebastian, September 6, 1746.

M. Sarah Sebastian and Timothy Lyons, January 11, 1746/7.

M. Joshua Sebastian and Priscilla Mirax, March 10, 1748/9.

B. Nicholas, son of Richard and Elizabeth Sebastian, February 15, 1749/50.

M. Alice Sebastian and Andrew Allen, February 12, 1750/1.

M. Thomas Elliot Sebastian and Frances Embry, June 4, 1751.

M. Joseph Sebastian and Anne Coventry, September 8, 1751.

M. Mary Sebastian and Benjamin Suddith, February 24, 1752.

M. Francis Selph and Elizabeth Gravat, October 16, 1763.

M. John Selvie and Elizabeth Thomson, June 29, 1727.

        SETTLE : SETTLES : SUTTLE : SUTTLES : SUTTELS

M. Isaac Suttle and Charity Brown of Hanover Parish, September 24, 1726,
    "per certification from under the Clerk of the Church's hand may appear."

M. Elizabeth Suttle of Hanover Parish and John McCormick, March 8, 1735/6.

M. Verlinda Suttle and Joel Ancrom, September 12, 1745.

B. Henry, son of William and Hannah Suttels, September 20, 1769.

M. Thomas Settle and Elizabeth Wharton, February 26, 1778.

M. Hannah Settle and William Massey, February 8, 1784.

M. Elizabeth Settles and Thomas Tyler, January 5, 1787. [King George County
    Marriage Register records a license for the marriage of Thomas Taylor
    and Elizabeth Settles.]

M. Reuben Settle and Mary Taylor, June 15, 1792.

B. Margaret, daughter of Margaret Sharer, March 12, 1736/7.

B. Patrick, son of Margaret Sharer, September 14, 1741.

M. Margaret Sharer and Thomas Fletcher, December 26, 1744.

D. Thomas Sharpe's wife and child, January 28, 1723/4.

D. Thomas Sharp, April 4, 1726.

D. Thomas Sharp, December 1, 1734.

M. Frances Sharp of this Parish and John Kendall of Washington Parish, December 22, 1737.

D. John Sharp, February 3, 1741/2.

M. Sarah Sharpe and William Elliot, December 17, 1752.

M. Elizabeth Sharp and Vincent Kelly, January 26, 1769.

M. Patrick Sheerman and Anne Joy, August 9, 1768.

M. Isaac Shepherd and Martha Greenslet, February 17, 1749/50.

SHEVRY : SHIVEREL   SEE: SACHEVEREL &c. Page 118

B. John, son of Margaret Shipton, June 25, 1738.

B. Mary, daughter of John and Theodocia Short, November 17, 1745.

B. Thomas, son of John and Theodocia Short, February 9, 1746/7.

B. Sarah, daughter of John Short, January 14, 1748/9.

B. Elizabeth, daughter of John and Theodosia Short, July 8, 1757.

B. Anne, daughter of John and Theodosia Short, January 17, 1760.

B. Thomas, son of John and [blank] Short, August 16, 1761.

B. John, son of John and Theodosia Short, May 1, 1763.

M. Mary Short and Benjamin Harrison, November 17, 1770.

M. Sarah Short and Sigismund Massey, July 16, 1772.

M. Elizabeth Short and William Bunbury, January 16, 1783.

M. John Shotwell and Sarah Worldey, June 26, 1725.

B. Jeremiah, son of John and Sarah Shotwell, June 16, 1726.

M. Mary Shropshire of Hanover Parish and Joseph Smith, April 3, 1746.

SIDEBOTTOM : SIDEBUTTEN

B. Thomas, son of Peter and Sary Sidebutten, January 7, 1736/7.

B. [Blank], son of Peter and Sarah Sidebottom, October 18, 1741.

B. William, son of Peter and Sarah Sidebottom, August 17, 1743.

B. Charles, son of Peter and Sarah Sidebottom, March 3, 1745/6.

B. Peter, a free mulatto, son of Peter and Sarah Sidebottom, April 9, 1748.

B. Anne, daughter of Peter and Sarah Sidebottom, August 18, 1758.

B. Sarah, daughter of William and Elizabeth Sidebottom, June 8, 1767.

B. Thomas, son of William and Elizabeth Sidebottom, February 19, 1769.

M. Martha Sill and Peter Nugent, both of Hanover Parish, February 15, 1731/2.

B. Sarah, daughter of John and Jane Silver, December 18, 1745.

D. John, son of Matthew and Elizabeth Simmons, October 1, 1720.

B. Matthias, son of Matthias and Mary Simmons, December 5, 1725.

M. Mary Simmons and Philip Crafford, November 27, 1730.

M. Ephraim Simmons and Mary Pew, April 13, 1740.

M. Duncan Simson and Jane Dinsford, December 27, 1732.

B. Samuel, son of Duncan and Jane Simson, March 7, 1734/5.

M. John Simpson of Overwharton Parish and Elizabeth Naylor of Brunswick Parish, August 6, 1735.

B. Duncan, son of Samuel and Lettice Simpson, January 13, 1764.

B. Samuel Fetherington, son of Samuel Simpson, December 15, 1765.

B. William, son of Samuel and Elizabeth Simpson, July 21, 1768.

M. Elizabeth Simpson and William Briant, June 21, 1779.

M. Samuel Sims and Sarah Macnall, July 10, 1735.

M. James Sims and Elizabeth Embry, October 14, 1762.

M. Sarah Sims and James Baxter, October 20, 1764.

B. Elisha, son of Mary Anne Sims, March 26, 1766.

M. Victory Simms and Ambrose Deakins, May 24, 1789.

M. Margaret Skerry and Thomas Kelton, December 24, 1726

SKIDMORE   SEE: SCUDAMORE

M. Sarah Skidmore and George Spicer, July 1, 1744.

B. Hannah, daughter of Jemima Skidmore, March 19, 1746/7.

M. William Skidmore and Elizabeth Bowin, May 11, 1747.

M. Elizabeth Skidmore and John Ducket, August 6, 1751.

M. Joshua Skidmore and Frances Bush, August 6, 1751.

M. Jemima Skidmore and Joseph Suddith, August 18, 1751.

B. Sarah, daughter of Joshua and Frances Skidmore, December 22, 1754.

B. William, son of Adam and Catherine Skinner, September 22, 1716.

D. William, son of Adam and [blank] Skinner, January 20, 1716/7.

B. Allin, daughter of Adam and Allin Skinner, August 12, 1722.

D. Allin, daughter of Adam and Allin Skinner, September 19, 1722.

M. Penelope Skinner and Archibald Allen, December 26, 1722.

B. Mary, daughter of Adam and Catherine Skinner [mutilated], 1724.

Baptized Thomas, son of Adam and Catherine Skinner, April 9, 1727.

B. Katherine, daughter of Adam and Katherine Skinner, April 5, 1732.

B. William, son of Katherine Skinner, April 19, 1737.

M. Katherine Skinner and Thomas Adams, October 18, 1738.

M. John Skinner and Sarah Roe, September 15, 1743.

B. Thomas, son of John and Sarah Skinner, November 9, 1746.

B. Henry Savin, son of John and Sarah Skinner, September 26, 1749.

M. Thomas Skinner and Mary Elliot, December 26, 1749.

B. John, son of John and Sarah Skinner, January 30, 1752.

M. William Skinner and Anne Heaps, August 20, 1767.

M. Adah Skinner and John Sullivan, April 17, 1788.

M. Leah Skinner and Henry Mehorner, September 13, 1788.

M. Zilpah Skinner and Thomas Truslow, January 19, 1789.

M. James Smallwood and Frances Sweney, May 23, 1776.

B. Mary, daughter of John and Charity Smith, November 11, 1716.

M. John Smith and Mary Anchrum, February 17, 1717/8.

B. Mary, daughter of John and Sarah Smith, Deceased, September 7, 1722.

D. Sarah Smith, September 17, 1722.

M. Anne Smith and Richard Wilson, October 31, 1722.

M. John Smith and Mary Duncan, November 15, 1722.

M. Henry Smith and Margaret Chrystie, May 28, 1723.

M. Alice Smith and Edward Thomson, December 4, 1723.

B. John, son of John and Sarah Smith, August 14, 1725.

M. John Smith and Pleasant Rose, September 30, 1725.

D. Matthew Smith, December 10, 1725.

M. Elizabeth Smith and Edward McDonald, February 6, 1735/6.

D. Margaret Smith, August 17, 1728.

M. John Smith and Margaret Grigsby, November 5, 1728.

M. Henry Smith and Margaret Spicer, September 23, 1729.

M. Sarah Smith and John Ben Gregg, June 22, 1730.

M. Elizabeth Smith and John White, November 12, 1730.

B. Anne, daughter of John and Margaret Smith, September 2, 1731.

B. Mary, daughter of Henry and Margaret Smith, July 15, 1732.

D. Margaret Smith, April 13, 1733.

M. Henry Smith and Jane Kelly, September 24, 1733.

B. Edward, son of Henry and Jane Smith, June 20, 1734.

D. Mary, daughter of Henry and Margaret Smith, November 15, 1734.

B. Charles, son of John and Margaret Smith, September 20, 1735.

D. Peter Smith, December 28, 1735.

M. Elizabeth Smith and Edward McDonald, February 6, 1735/6.

D. Sarah Smith, May 24, 1736.

D. John, son of John Smith, June 26, 1736.

B. John, son of Henry and Jane Smith, April 7, 1737.

B. Sarah, daughter of John and Margaret Smith, July 14, 1738.

B. Sarah, daughter of Henry and Jane Smith, February 10, 1739/40.

B. John, son of John and Margaret Smith, October 3, 1740.

B. Henry, son of John and Margaret Smith, June 15, 1742.

B. Elizabeth, daughter of Henry and Jane Smith, August 11, 1743.

B. Katherine, daughter of John and Margaret Smith, November 18, 1743.

B. Kijah, daughter of Joseph and Elizabeth Smith, December 21, 1743.

B. Margaret Smith, April 18, 1745.

M. Jemima Smith of Washington Parish and William Monroe, April 2, 1746.

M. Joseph Smith and Mary Shropshire of Hanover Parish, April 3, 1746.

B. John, son of John and Margaret Smith, July 19, 1746.

D. Jane, wife of Henry Smith, November 21, 1748.

M. John Smith and Anne Yarentharp, March 7, 1748/9.

M. Henry Smith and Hester Stone, May 21, 1749.

B. Mildred, daughter of John and Elizabeth Smith, March 22, 1752.

B. William, son of William and Elizabeth Smith, August 13, 1752.

M. Anne Smith and Charles Christie, March 18, 1753.

M. Henry Smith and Elizabeth Jackson, July 11, 1753.

B. Mary, daughter of Henry and Elizabeth Smith, October 13, 1755.

M. Henry Smith, Junior, and Sarah Johnson, March 19, 1756.

B. Jane, daughter of Henry and Sarah Smith, April 2, 1756.

B, Charles, son of William and Elizabeth Smith, December 12, 1757.

B. Mildred, daughter of William and Sarah Smith, April 17, 1758.

M. Margaret Smith and John Day, May 15, 1758.

B. Mildred, daughter of Charles and Sarah Smith, January 1, 1759.

M. Charles Smith and Sarah Grigg, January 20, 1759.

B. Winifred, daughter of Henry and Elizabeth Smith, November 20, 1759.

M. Elizabeth Smith and Richard McLachlan, January 31, 1760.

B. Catherine, daughter of George and Behethland Smith, March 24, 1760.

B. Jacob, son of Henry and Sarah Smith, December 3, 1760.

B. Margaret, daughter of Charles and Sarah Smith, March 4, 1761.

B. Mary, daughter of John and Elizabeth Smith, May 13, 1761.

B. Sarah, daughter of George Smith, March [blank], 1762.

B. Charles, son of Charles and Sarah Smith, May 27, 1764.

B. Winifred, daughter of Charles and Sarah Smith, December 10, 1765.

M. John Smith and Anne Ball, December 26, 1765.

B. Margaret, daughter of John and Anne Smith, November 20, 1766.

M. Henry Smith and Sarah Leech, December 29, 1767.

M. Elizabeth Smith and William Lewis Murphey, April 5, 1768.

M. Charles Smith and Anne Griggs, January 24, 1769.

B. Letitia, daughter of Charles and Anne Smith, July 15, 1771.

B. Behethland, daughter of George and Behethland Smith, April 16, 1772.

B. Margaret, daughter of Charles and Anne Smith, February 9, 1772.

B. Sarah, daughter of Henry and Sarah Smith, June 12, 1774.

M. Mildred Smith and Thomas Brown, December 16, 1773.

M. John Smith and Mary Stribling, January 8, 1778.

M. Henry Smith and Anne Gutridge, July 17, 1778.

M. Jacob Smith and Ann Johnston, November 1, 1781.

M. Nathan Smith and Betsy Washington, April 4, 1790.

M. William Smoot and Frances Bunbury, September 23, 1775.

M. Thomas South and Dorothy Buckley, July 10, 1753.

B. William, son of Thomas and Dorothy South, August 3, 1754.

D. William Sowel, October 23, 1725.

B. Katherine, daughter of Hannah Sowel, February 2, 1726/7.

M. Molly Sparkes and John Henneage, October 22, 1785.

M. Lettice Speerman of Washington Parish and John Douling, May 1, 1746.

M. Sarah Spicer and William Burton, December 14, 1725.

M. Rachel Spicer and Isaac Sebastian, May 11, 1727.

M. Margaret Spicer and Henry Smith, September 23, 1729.

B. William, son of William and Elizabeth Spicer, April 6, 1732.

M. Anne Spicer of this Parish and John Clanton of Hanover Parish,
    February 17, 1731/2.

B. Lettice, daughter of William and Margaret Spicer, January 20, 1733/4.

M. Benjamin Spicer and Rose Grigsby, June 6, 1734.

M. Joseph Spicer and Margaret Swillivan, September 14, 1741.

M. George Spicer and Sarah Skidmore, July 1, 1744.

M. Lettice Spicer and Francis Fletcher, November 8, 1745.

M. Elizabeth Spiler and William Bruton, June 5, 1725.

D. George Spiller, May 21, 1718.

M. William Spilman and Mildred Duling, December 22, 1787.

B. John, son of Enoch and Grace Spinks, July 9, 1721.

M. John Spinks of Brunswick Parish and Rosamond Corbin of this Parish,
    November 6, 1741.

B. Elizabeth, daughter of John and Rosamand Spinks, August 18, 1745.

B. William, son of Mary Stanford, November 3, 1720.

D. William, son of Mary Stanford, February 1, 1720/1.

M. James Staples and Jane Owens, February 12, 1778.

M. William Staples and Frances Raulet, February 18, 1790. [King George County Marriage Register records a license issued to William Staples and Frances Rawlett which is the usual spelling of the name.]

M. Anne Steed and John Story, February 18, 1759.

M. William Steel and Anne Prestridge, April 27, 1742.

M. John Stephens and Mary Whiting, February 24, 1725/6.

B. John, son of John and Elizabeth Stephens, December 5, 1726.

M. Jarret Stevens and Margaret Elkins, June 21, 1727.

M. William Stevenson and Mary Collins, September 24, 1761.

M. Catherine Stiglar and Robert Stringfellow, May 15, 1762.

M. Elizabeth Stith and Henry Fitzhugh, October 28, 1770.

M. Buckner Stith and Anne Dade, February 26, 1772.

B. Baldwin Buckner, son of Buckner Stith and Anne, his wife, February 3, 1773.

M. Robert Stith and Mary T. Washington, July 29, 1773.

M. John Stith and Anne Washington, December 11, 1783.

M. Griffin Stith and Frances Townshend Washington, June 14, 1788.

M. George Stone and Catherine Schofield, July 1, 1716.

D. Catherine Stone, January 25, 1725/6.

M. George Stone and Mary Toul, June 4, 1726.

D. Mary, wife of George Stone, January 10, 1726/7.

D. George Stone, March 12, 1726/7.

M. John Stone and Martha Davies, May 16, 1739.

B. Mary, daughter of John and Martha Stone, April 30, 1740.

M. Eli Stone and Rebecca Davis, December 4, 1746.

B. John, son of Eli and Rebecca Stone, November 18, 1748.

M. Hester Stone and Henry Smith, May 21, 1749.

M. Josias Stone and Margaret Cash, April 8, 1780.

B. Behethland, daughter of William and Elizabeth Storke, December 27, 1716.

B. Margaret, daughter of William and Elizabeth Storke, January 18, 1720/1.

B. Catherine, daughter of William and Elizabeth Storke, December 17, 1723.

B. John, son of William and Elizabeth Storke, July 11, 1725.

M. Elizabeth Storke and Richard Bernard, August 29, 1729.

M. Behethlem Storke of this Parish and Anthony Strother of St.George's
    Parish, August 25, 1733.

M. Margaret Storke and John Washington, November 23, 1738.

M. Elizabeth Storke and Henry Washington, Junior, May 18, 1743.

M. Catherine Storke and Bailey Washington, January 12, 1748/9.

M. John Storke and Frances Hooe, March 21, 1750/1.

B. William, son of John and Frances Storke, September 25, 1753.

M. John Story and Anne Steed, February 18, 1759.

M. Mary Stoward and William Scaplehorn, February 21, 1754.

D. Hugh Strahan, April 11, 1745.

B. Clarinda, daughter of William and Sarah Strange, March 1, 1766.

M. Sarah Stransford and Anthony Lucas, November 4, 1737.

    STRATTON : STRAUTTON

M. Benoni Strautton and Anne Derrick, December 24, 1733.

B. Frances, daughter of Benoni and Anne Stratton, October 18, 1734.

B. Thomas Derrick, son of Benoni and Anne Stratton, November 3, 1736.

B. Katherine, daughter of Benoni and Anne Stratton, February 13, 1738/9.

B. Susanna, daughter of Benoni Stratton, March 5, 1740/1.

B. William, son of Benoni Stratton, April [blank], 1742.

B. Benoni, son of Benoni Stratton, August 22, 1744.

M. Anne Stratton and John Eddeson, July 12, 1751.

M. Frances Stratton and William Lord, October 31, 1756.

M. Benoni Stratton and Elizabeth Lewis, September 29, 1772.

STRIBLING : STRIPLING : STRIBLIN : STRIPLIN

B. Margaret, daughter of Benjamin Stripling, January 11 and died January 12, 1715/6.

B. Benjamin and Anne, son and daughter of Joel and Mary Stripling, May 31, 1716.

D. Joel Stripling, September 14, 1718.

M. Joel Stribling and Hester Colclough, September 25, 1723.

M. Thomas Stribling and Elizabeth Newton, December 7, 1725.

B. Newton, son of Thomas and Elizabeth Striblin, November 11, 1726.

B. Thomas, son of Thomas and Elizabeth Striblin, April 20, 1728.

D. Elizabeth Striblin, May 12, 1728.

M. Sarah Stribling and Peter Ker, August 23, 1728.

B. Colclough, son of Joel and Hester Stribling, [torn and mutilated], circa 1728-1729.

M. Thomas Stribling and Jane Thomas, November 17, 1729.

B. William, son of Thomas and Jane Stribling, January 20, 1730/1.

B. Hester, daughter of Joel and Hester Stribling, April 5, 1732.

B. Frances, daughter of Thomas and Jane Stribling, June 20, 1734.

B. Bradford, son of Joel and Hester Stribling, January 11, 1735/6.

B. Jane, daughter of Thomas and Jane Stribling, January 21, 1736/7.

M. Anne Stribling of this Parish and Bushrod Dogged of Brunswick Parish, October 6, 1737.

D. Joel Stribling, March 19, 1737/8.

B. Mary, daughter of Joel and Hester Stribling, November 4, 1738.

B. Elizabeth, daughter of Thomas and Jane Stribling, September 18, 1739.

B. Anne, daughter of Thomas and Jane Stribling, January 18, 1741/2.

D. Benjamin Stribling, February 10, 1742/3.

B. Margaret, daughter of Thomas and Jane Stribling, March 10, 1743/4.

M. Hester Stribling and Thomas Lewis Parrat, April 16, 1744.

D. Joel, son of Joel and Hester Stribling, September 27, 1744.

B. Milly, daughter of Thomas and Jane Stribling, January 28, 1747/8.

M. Cochley [Colclough] Striblin and Mary Hodge, October 6, 1749.

B. Mary, daughter of Thomas and Jane Stribling, September 17, 1750.

M. Thomas Stribling and Elizabeth Peck, March 8, 1752.

B. Newton, son of Thomas and Elizabeth Stribling, October 10, 1752.

M. William Stribling and Elizabeth Derrick, January 7, 1753.

B. Joel, son of Colchley and Frances Stribling, March 11, 1753.

B. Jemima, daughter of William and Elizabeth Stribling, March 26, 1753.

B. Sarah, daughter of Thomas and Jane Stribling, May 17, 1753.

B. William, son of William and Elizabeth Stribling, March 28, 1755.

M. Hester Stribling and Francis Rose, May 31, 1756.

B. Benjamin, son of Colchley and Frances Stribling, June 15, 1756.

B. Joel, son of Thomas and Jane Stribling, August 17, 1756.

B. Winifred, daughter of William and Elizabeth Stribling, July 20, 1757.

B. Joel, son of Colclough and Frances Stribling, March 8, 1758.

M. Jane Stribling and John Curry, September 20, 1758.

B. William Derrick, son of William and Elizabeth Stribling, June 12, 1759.

B. John Colclough, son of Colclough and Frances Stribling, January 5, 1760.

B. Thomas, son of William and Elizabeth Stribling, February 9, 1761.

B. Jemima, daughter of William and Elizabeth Stribling, January 29, 1764.

B. Susanna, daughter of Colclough and Frances Stribling, April 27, 1764.

M. [Blank] Stribling and Reuben Burgess, September 1, 1765.

B. Thomas, son of Colclough and Frances Stribling, October 22, 1766.

M. Elizabeth Stribling and Anthony Price, January 17, 1768.

B. Mary, daughter of Colclough and Frances Stribling, February 16, 1769.

M. Mildred Stribling and John Knowling, April 11, 1776.

M. Margaret Stribling and James Rallings, January 5, 1778.

M. Mary Stribling and John Smith, January 8, 1778.

B. Lucy, daughter of James and Susanna Stringfellow, January 11, 1761.

M. Robert Stringfellow and Catherine Stiglar, May 15, 1762.

B. Elizabeth, daughter of Robert and Catherine Stringfellow, January 29, 1768.

M. Anthony Strother of St. George's Parish and Behethlem Storke of this Parish, August 25, 1733.

M. Elizabeth Strother and Robert Kay, December 13, 1762.

M. Enoch Strother and Mary Kay, February 12, 1763.

M. Anne Strother and John James, September 16, 1763.

M. William Strother and Winifred Baker of Westmoreland County, September 26, 1765.

STRUTTON   SEE: STRATTON [Pages 131 and 132]

B. William, son of the Reverend David and Jane Stuart, December 13, 1723.

M. James Stuart and Margaret Reins, March 24, 1724/5.

B. Mary, daughter of the Reverend David and Jane Stuart, February 24, 1725/6.

B. John, son of the Reverend David and Jane Stuart, May 10, 1728.

B. Sarah, daughter of the Reverend David and Jane Stuart, February 21, 1730/1.

B. Charles, son of the Reverend David and Jane Stuart, April 16, 1733.

B. Frances, daughter of Joseph and Sarah Stuart, November 1, 1735.

M. Alexander Stuart and Mary Turner, December 23, 1739.

B. Margaret, daughter of Alexander and Mary Stuart, April 17, 1742.

M. Mary Stuart and Sigismond Massey, April 4, 1743.

D. Alexander Stuart, January 24, 1742/3.

M. Mary Stuart and James Boswel, April 6, 1744.

D. The Reverend David Stuart, Rector of Saint Paul's Parish, January 31, 1748/9.

D. Mrs. Jane Stuart, Relict of ye Reverend David Stuart, January 14, 1749/50.

M. John Stuart and Frances Alexander, February 16, 1749/50.

M. Sarah Stuart and Thomas Fitzhugh, June 19, 1750.

B. William Gibbons, son of John and Frances Stuart, November 25, 1750.

M. William Stuart and Sarah Foote, November 26, 1750.

B. Jane, daughter of William and Sarah Stuart, December 1, 1751.

B. Philip, son of John and Frances Stuart, February 18, 1752.

M. Charles Stuart and Frances Washington, February 23, 1752.

M. Charles Stuart of King George County and Susanna Grigsby, November 9, 1752.

B. David, son of William and Sarah Stuart, August 3, 1753.

B. John, son of Charles and Frances Stuart, September 22, 1753.

M. Charles Stuart and Frances Dade, August 6, 1754.

B. Martha, daughter of John and Frances Stuart, October 10, 1754.

B. John, son of John and Frances Stuart, March 1, 1757.

B. John Alexander, son of John and Frances Stuart, April 20, 1758.

B. Elizabeth, daughter of Charles and Frances Stuart, November 15, 1758.

B. Mary, daughter of Charles and Frances Stuart, December 22, 1760.

B. Philip, son of John and Frances Stuart, February 22, 1761.

B. William, son of William and Sarah Stuart, October 21, 1761.

B. Henry Foote, son of William and Sarah Stuart, April 25, 1763.

B. Charles, son of John and Frances Stuart, August 23, 1763.

B. Richard, son of William and Sarah Stuart, September 4, 1770.

M. Jane Stuart and Townshend Dade, December 11, 1769.

B. Henry Foote, son of William and Sarah Stuart, October 18, 1772.

M. Martha Stuart and William Thornton, May 11, 1775.

B. Jane, daughter of William and Sarah Stuart, May 15, 1776.

M. Price Stuart and Ann Clifton, October 17, 1781.

M. Charles Stuart and Helen Wray, October 31, 1783.

M. John Alexander Stuart and Mary Wray, November 17, 1785.

D. Henry Foote, son of the Reverend William Stuart and Sarah, his wife, June 8, 1793.

M. Anne Stuart and William Mason, July 11, 1793.

M. Jane Stuart and Richard Foote, December 16, 1795.

D. Reverend William Stuart, October 1, 1798, aged 75 years, "after a tedious confinement with the Gout. [signed] Richard Stuart."

SUDDATH : SUDDITH : SUDDUTH :   SEE: SUTHARD [Page 138]

M. John Suthard and Frances Carver, June 8, 1733.

M. Joseph Sudduth and Margaret Sebastian, October 13, 1735.

B. John, son of John and Frances Suthard, April 21, 1736.

M. Rose Sudduth and John Kennedy, June 21, 1736.

B. Lettice, daughter of John and Frances Sudduth, July 6, 1738.

B. Mary, daughter of John and Frances Sudduth, August 21, 1740.

D. Margaret, wife of Joseph Sudduth, November 3, 1741.

M. Robert Sudduth, Junior, and Sarah Walker, January 26, 1741/2.

M. Sarah Sudduth and James Grigsby, May 9, 1742.

B. Joseph, son of Robert and Sarah Sudduth, November 2, 1742.

B. Joseph, son of Joseph and Frances Sudduth, November 8, 1742.

B. William, son of John and Frances Sudduth, March 9, 1744/5.

B. Elizabeth, daughter of John and Frances Sudduth, March 14, 1744/5.

B. Mary, daughter of Robert and Sarah Sudduth, January 16, 1746/7.

B. Sarah, daughter of Robert and Sarah Sudduth, September 7, 1748.

M. Hannah Sudduth and John Hall, November 6, 1749.

M. Absolom Suddath and Sarah Elliot, October 2, 1750.

M. Robert Suddath and Elizabeth Cooper, October 2, 1750.

M. Joseph Suddith and Jemima Skidmore, August 18, 1751.

M. Benjamin Suddith and Mary Sebastian, February 24, 1752.

B. Benjamin, son of Benjamin and Mary Suddith, March 1, 1757.

B. Isaac, son of Benjamin and Margaret Suddith, July 6, 1760.

B. William, son of Robert and Sarah Suddith, August 5, 1764.

M. Lettice Suthard and John Culham, February 17, 1775.

SULLIVAN : SULYVAN : SWILLIVAN   SEE: SWILLAKEEN [Page 139]

B. William, son of Mary Sullivan, belonging to the Estate of Colonel
    William Fitzhugh, January 12, 1721/2.

M. Helenor Sulyvan and Hugh McCarty, April 22, 1730.

M. Margaret Sullivan and Joseph Spicer, September 14, 1741.

M. Burgess Swillivan and Anne Carver, February 3, 1747/8.

B. Sallis, daughter of Burgess and Anne Sulyvan, October 24, 1748.

B. William, son of Burgess and Anne Sullivan, October 8, 1750.

B. Harry, son of Burgess and Anne Swillivan, July 6, 1758.

M. Mildred Sullivan and William Coheley, February 4, 1781.

M. John Sullivan and Adah Skinner, April 17, 1788.

M. Michael Summers and Hannah Edwards, May 12, 1724.

B. Mary, daughter of Michael and Hannah Sommers, April 3, 1728.

B. John and Jemima, son and daughter of Michael and Hannah Summers,
    July 16, 1732.

B. Sarah, daughter of Michael and Hannah Summers, July 20, 1735.

B. Margaret, daughter of Michael and Hannah Summers, June 14, 1738.

B. Elizabeth, daughter of Michael and Susanna Summers, December 5, 1740.

B. Anne, daughter of Michael and Susanna Summers, June 22, 1744.

B. Samuel, son of Michael and Susanna Summers, November 1, 1746.

B. Susanna, daughter of Michael and Hannah Summers, July 25, 1748.

M. Margaret Sumner of Overwharton Parish and John Minor of Brunswick Parish, February 3, 1740/1.*

M. Lettice Súmner and James Hansbury, September 19, 1741. [See Page 62]*

SUTHARD : SUDDERD   SEE: SUDDATH &c. Page 136

B. Absolom, son of Robert and Diana Sudderd, February 21, 1725/6

B. Hannah, daughter of Robert and Diana Suthard, May 2, 1728.

B. Moses, son of Robert and Diana Suthard, September 22, 1732.

M. Lettice Suthard and John Culham, February 17, 1775.

M. Anne Sutherland and Gustavus Elgin, March 26, 1793.
    SUTTLE   SEE: SETTLE &C. Page 122
M. John Sutton and Martha Kenneman, September 17, 1723.

D. Marthy Sutton, December 10, 1725.

M. Thomas Sweatman and Frances Call, December 16, 1765.

SWEENY : SWENEY

M. Paul Sweeny and Frances Williams, December 24, 1728.

B. Sarah, daughter of Paul and Frances Sweeny, October 23, 1731.

M. Sarah Sweney and Peter Culvy, March 28, 1758.

M. Sarah Sweney and Elias Rose, September 2, 1758.

M. Elizabeth Sweney and James Jackson, December 31, 1767.

---

*   Joseph Sumner, Junior, Gentleman, of Overwharton Parish, had three only children, the above mentioned Margaret and Lettice Sumner and Elizabeth Sumner who married Peter Mauzey. These ladies were heiresses to his 1200 acre plantation in Stafford County. Peter Hansbrough (1744-1822), son of James and Lettice Hansbrough, married September 10, 1766, his first cousin Eleanor Minor (1744-1812), daughter of John and Margaret Minor; he died testate in Culpeper County, Virginia, possessed of a handsome landed estate in the counties of Stafford, King George and Culpeper.

M. John Sweney and Margaret Addason, October 6, 1769.

M. Frances Sweney and James Smallwood, May 23, 1776.

M. Susanna Sweney and William Burke, February 1, 1778.

   SWILLAKEEN   SEE: SULLIVAN : SULYVAN : SWILLIVAN [PAGE 137]

M. Anne Swillakeen and John Rose, January 4, 1776.

                                T

D. Robert Taliaferro, June 6, 1726.

M. Richard Taliaferro of Essex County and Rose Berryman of this county,
    June 10, 1726.

M. Frances Taliaferro and Kenelm Cheseldine, August 9, 1768.

M. John Taliaferro and Lucy Alexander, January 24, 1774.

M. Lawrence Taliaferro and Sarah Dade, February 3, 1774.

M. James Talmash and Mary Clark, May 17, 1792.

M. George Tavener and Elizabeth Bishop, January 2, 1739/40.

B. Elizabeth, daughter of George and Elizabeth Taven[er], September 11,
    1740.

B. John, son of John and Anne Taylor, August 20, 1718.

M. John Taylor and Mary Moss, August 19, 1724.

D. Mary Taylor, March 25, 1726.

M. John Taylor and Mary Ancrom, February 27, 1726/7.

B. William, son of John and Mary Taylor, March 23, 1727/8.

D. Mary Taylor, October 21, 1732.

M. John Taylor and Verlinda Dunahoo, December 13, 1776.

M. Sarah Taylor and Zachariah Rose, March 19, 1778.
*
M. Mary Taylor and Reuben Settle, July 15, 1792.

M. Daniel Taylour and Sarah Carver, January 19, 1764.

---

*   For Thomas Taylor see Thomas Tyler, page 145.

B. Jane, daughter of Edward and Sarah Templeman, December 7, 1747.

B. Mary, daughter of Henry and Susanna Tennison, April 7, 1718.

D. Mary, daughter of Henry and Susanna Tennyson, September 11, 1718.

D. Susanna Tennyson, April 4, 1720.

B. Mary, daughter of Henry and Anne Tennyson, August 9, 1721.

B. Richard, son of Daniel and Anne Ternan, November 25, 1745.

B. John, son of Richard and Sarah Thomas, November 10, 1717.

M. William Thomas and Thomason Ham, December 22, 1724.

D. William Thomas, June 2, 1725.

B. Anne, daughter of William and Thomison Thomas, November 5, 1725.

M. Mary Thomas and John Ancrom, January 27, 1726/7.

B. Virolinda, daughter of William and Thomason Thomas, April 20, 1728.

M. Jane Thomas and Thomas Stribling, November 17, 1729.

B. Anthony Buckner, son of Jane Kelly alias Thomas, April 30, 1731.

M. Massey Thomas and Mary Price, November 28, 1731.

B. John, son of Massey and Mary Thomas, April 26, 1732.

B. Anne, daughter of William and Thomison Thomas, December 12, 1733.

B. William, son of Massey and Mary Thomas, October 12, 1734.

B. Sarah, daughter of Massey and Mary Thomas, September 28, 1737.

B. George, son of Massey and Mary Thomas, February 28, 1738/9.

B. Milly, daughter of William and Theozen Thomas, December 15, 1739.

B. Anne, daughter of Massey and Mary Thomas, March 15, 1740/1.

M. John Thomas and Jemima Derrick, August 10, 1741.

B. Sarah, daughter of John and Jemima Thomas, April 10, 1742.

B. Mary, daughter of John and Jemima Thomas, May 26, 1744.

B. William, son of John and Jemima Thomas, November 10, 1746.

D. Richard Thomas, December 3, 1748.

M. Sarah Thomas and Lovel White, December 14, 1749.

B. Jane, daughter of John and Jemima Thomas, July 19, 1750.

M. William Thomas and Jane Johnson, December 25, 1752.

B. Susanna, daughter of William and Sarah Thomas, February 3, 1755.

M. Anthony Buckner Thomas and Amy Powel, April 20, 1755.

B. Elizabeth, daughter of William and Sarah Thomas, October 7, 1757.

M. Sarah Thomas and John Gray, May 11, 1758.

M. John Thomas and Mary Thomas, February 19, 1762.

M. Jane Thomas and Thomas King, May 19, 1771.

M. Price Thomas and Mary Monroe, November 7, 1779.

M. Mary Thomas and Aaron Mardus, March 12, 1785.

M. William Thomas and Mary White, December 13, 1785.

D. Ruth, daughter of Elizabeth Thompson, May 18, 1718.

D. William Thompson, December 30, 1725.

M. William Thompson and Jane Holland, December 26, 1765.

B. James, son of William and Jane Thompson, February 24, 1768.

B. Sarah, daughter of William and Sarah Thompson, August 5, 1769.

B. William, son of William and Sarah Thompson, June 14, 1772.

B. Jane, daughter of William and Jane Thompson, September 29, 1774.

M. Margaret Thompson and William Christie, June 6, 1775.

M. Sarah Thompson and Dennis Mehorner, February 21, 1781.

M. William Thompson and Anne Washington, August 3, 1785.

M. Andrew Thompson and Mary Rose, January 2, 1787.

M. Edward Thomson and Alice Smith, December 4, 1723.

M. Richard Thomson and Elizabeth Oxford, June 3, 1724.

M. James Thomson and Elizabeth Armour, August 10, 1724.

B. James, son of James and Elizabeth Thomson, November 15, 1726.

M. Elizabeth Thomson and John Selvie, June 29, 1727.

D. Edward Thomson, September 24, 1728.

THORNBERY : THORNBERRY : THORNBURY

D. Richard Thornberry, September 11, 1716.

M. Mary Thornberry of Saint Paul's Parish and William Horton of King
George County, January 12, 1741/2.

M. Samuel Thornbery and Mary Kidwell, April 20, 1744.

B. John Kidwell, son of Samuel and Mary Thornbery, February 19, 1744/5.

B. Elizabeth, daughter of Samuel and Mary Thornbery, April 15, 1746.

B. William, son of William and Elizabeth Thornbury, March 20, 1748/9.

M. John Thornbury and Elizabeth Bolling, December 14, 1749.

B. Harry, son of John and Elizabeth Thornbury, July 12, 1750.

B. John, son of John and Elizabeth Thornbury, January 3, 1752.

B. Peggy, daughter of John and Elizabeth Thornbury, October 5, 1753.

B. John Deneal, son of William and Elizabeth Thornbury, December 4, 1753.

B. Mary, daughter of John and Elizabeth Thornberry, November 4, 1757.

B. William, son of John and Elizabeth Thornberry, October 10, 1760.

B. Francis, son of Anthony and Winifred Thornton, July 20, 1725.

B. Anthony, son of Anthony and Winifred Thornton, November 15, 1727.

M. Elizabeth Thornton and John Ford, January 27, 1729/30.

B. Judith Presley, daughter of Anthony and Winifred Thornton, October 3,
1731.

D. Judith Presley, daughter of Captain Anthony and Winifred Thornton,
October 11, 1733.

B. Peter, son of Anthony and Winifred Thornton, March 29, 1734.

M. Francis Thornton and Sarah Fitzhugh, April 2, 1747.

B. Winifred, daughter of Anthony and Sarah Thornton, January 14, 1747/8.

M. Winifred Thornton and William Bernard, November 25, 1750.

B. Sarah, daughter of Francis and Sarah Thornton, February 10, 1752.

M. William Thornton and Elizabeth Fitzhugh, April 26, 1757.

B. Susanna, daughter of William and Susanna Thornton, March 29, 1758.

B. William, son of Francis and Sarah Thornton, May 28, 1758.

M. John Thornton and Behethland Gilson Berryman, December 13, 1761.

M. Anthony Thornton and Susanna Fitzhugh, January 5, 1764.

M. Winifred Thornton and Daniel McCarty, January 13, 1765.

M. George Thornton and Mary Alexander, October 9, 1773.

M. William Thornton and Martha Stuart, May 11, 1775.

M. Lucy Thornton and John Brooke, July 2, 1777.

M. Presley Thornton and Elizabeth Thornton, March 26, 1784.

M. Presley Thornton and Alice Thornton, October 19, 1785.

M. Elizabeth Tilcock and James Hartly, April 1, 1768.

B. John, son of William and Mary Tilow [?], October 28, 1716.

M. Thomas Timons and Susanna Owens, May 14, 1749.

M. Mary Todd and John Murray, December 12, 1727.

B. William, son of Richard and Lucy Todd, February 12, 1727/8.

D. Richard Todd, January 18, 1736/7.

M. Lucy Todd and John Martin, November 5, 1742.

B. Samuel, son of Hayward and Sarah Todd, July 28, 1747.*

B. Hesther, daughter of Hayward and Mary Todd, April 13, 1750.

B. Lucy, daughter of Hayward and Sarah Todd, March 27, 1751.

---

*   This is the first entry in the Register in the handwriting of the
    Reverend William Stuart (1723-1798).

144   SAINT PAUL'S PARISH REGISTER

M. William Toul and Mary Porter, October 15, 1722.

M. Mary Toul and George Stone, June 4, 1726.

M. Elizabeth Townly and Richard Moody, February 5, 1758.

M. John Tracy of Washington Parish and Anne Coplee, August 7, 1740.

B. Luke, son of John and Anne Tracy, March 14, 1740/1.

B. James, son of John and Anne Tracy, February 12, 1744/5.

B. William, son of Thomas and Katherine Tratt, November 5, 1742.

M. Letitia Travers and James Grigsby, January 18, 1753.

B. Lucy, daughter of William and Margaret Travers, December 13, 1762.

M. John Travis and Margaret Hubart, June 28, 1722.

B. John, son of John and Anne Trayle, December 13, 1742.

M. Anne Tregar and William Chrismund, April 28, 1779.

M. Mary Trenar and Joseph Cook, December 26, 1723.

B. Anne, daughter of Mary Trigger, January 11, 1732/3.

M. Mary Trigger and William King, August 2, 1735.

M. William Trigger and Sarah Levi, February 1, 1786.

M. Mary Triplett and George Hibbill, February 12, 1728/9.

B. Francis, son of Francis and Susannah Triplett, February 12, 1732/3.

M. Benjamin Trusloe and Keziah Mannard, March 12, 1786. [King George County
    Marriage Register notes name of bride as Keziah Mannan.]

M. Thomas Truslow and Zilpah Skinner, January 19, 1789.

D. John Truyn, September 25, 1728.*

M. Joseph Tucker and Rosamond Carroll of Brunswick Parish, February 20,
    1733/4.

M. John Tunnel and Sarah Martin, February 18, 1763.

B. John, son of John and Sarah Turnel, August 29, 1767.

---

*   This may be John Fruyn; see page 53.

M. Mildred Tunnel and Woodford Kelly, February 4, 1769.

M. John Tunnel and Elizabeth Long, February 13, 1774.

M. Elizabeth Trunnel and William Sacheverel, February 26, 1784.

M. Richard Turner and Helena Carter, September 24, 1725.

D. Helenor Turner, October 11, 1739.

M. Mary Turner and Alexander Stuart, December 23, 1739.

M. John Turner and Sarah Derrick, October 2, 1741.

B. William, son of John and Sarah Turner, August 24, 1742.

B. John, son of John and Anne Turner, October 28, 1744.

B. Joseph, son of John and Sarah Turner, April 16, 1747.

M. Sarah Turner and John Norris, August 29, 1751.

M. John Turner and Martha Derrick, September 2, 1769.

B. William, son of John and Martha Turner, April 9, 1771.

B. Sarah, daughter of John and Martha Turner, September 6, 1772.

B. John Mattox, son of John and Martha Turner, December 16, 1774.

M. Thomas Tyler and Elizabeth Settles, January 5, 1787. [King George County Marriage Register records a license issued January 3, 1787 to Thomas Taylor and Elizabeth Settles.]

U

M. Fanny Underwood and John Lee, March 2, 1790.

V

M. William Vaint and Katherine Raddish, August 27, 1723.

B. Sarah, daughter of William and Catherine Vaint, July 3, 1725.

VINCENT : VINSON

M. Richard Vinson*and Grace Cheesman, December 31, 1730.

---

* The surname is written Winson here as well as in the next entry on page 146.

B. Cornelius, son of Richard and Grace Vinson, October 14, 1731.

B. Jane, daughter of Richard and Grace Vinson, June 23, 1733.

M. Jane Vinson and George Gregg, February 5, 1734/5.

M. Richard Vincent and Elizabeth Gregg, April 29, 1737.

B. William, son of Richard and Elizabeth Vincent, November 27, 1738.

D. Elizabeth, wife of Richard Vincent, December 2, 1738.

D. Richard Vincent, July 23, 1741.

M. Thomas Vincent and Elizabeth Pennal, April 3, 1749.

B. George, son of James and Elizabeth Vincent, April 10, 1749.

M. Rebecca Vowles and William Berryman, September 10, 1743.

W

M. Sarah Waemark and James Brown, May 11, 1760.

M. Mildred Wagstaff and George Hutcheson, September 19, 1727.

D. [Mutilated] Walker, April 20, 1717.

M. Ralph Walker and Sarah Bussee, January 26, 1722/3.

B. Martha, daughter of Ralph and Sarah Walker, August 15, 1725.

M. Sarah Walker and John Baker, October 30, 1725.

B. Mary, daughter of Richard and Elizabeth Walker, August 25, 1726.

B. Richard, son of Richard and Elizabeth Walker, April 17, 1732.

M. William Walker and Elizabeth Netherington, November 23, 1731.

B. Pellathye, daughter of Richard and Elizabeth Walker, February 23, 1734/5.

D. Thomas, son of Richard and Elizabeth Walker, November 4, 1735.

D. Elizabeth, wife of Richard Walker, November 6, 1735.

D. Elizabeth Walker, August 25, 1737.

M. Sarah Walker and Robert Sudduth, Junior, January 26, 1741/2.

B. William, son of William and Elizabeth Walker, March 25, 1744.

B. John, son of William and Elizabeth Walker, May 22, 1745.

B. James, son of William and Elizabeth Walker, October 16, 1746.

B. Elizabeth, daughter of William and Elizabeth Walker, December 22, 1747.

M. Elizabeth Walker and James McCant, March 15, 1747/8.

B. William, son of Richard and Eleanour Walker, March 15, 1749/50.

M. Mary Walker and John Hallet, August 1, 1751.

B. Jane, daughter of Eleanor Walker, July 28, 1756.

M. Mary Walker and James McDuff, March 3, 1757.

M. Anne Walpole and James Hartly, August 26, 1778.

M. George Nailour Waple and Mary Griffith, July 26, 1792.

M. Lurina Ward of this Parish and Henry Mintoe of Overwharton Parish, January 16, 1737/8.

M. William Ward and Margaret Fauman, December 24, 1741.

B. Mary, daughter of William and Margaret Ward, September 30, 1742.

D. Margaret, wife of William Ward, December 11, 1742.

B. Henry, son of Mary Ward, December 5, 1747.

B. Peggy, daughter of Mary Ward, February 19, 1750/1.

B. Sarah, daughter of Mary Ward, September 19, 1753.

M. William Ward and Elizabeth Jordan, December 25, 1753.

M. Henry Ward and Mary Rankins, June 14, 1775.

M. James Ward and Anne Willis, June 29, 1777.

B. Edward, son of Alexander and Alice Ware, March 20, 1715/6. [? 1716/7]

D. Edward, son of Alexander and Alice Ware, August 9, 1717.

D. Alexander Ware, [mutilated; in October or Novermber], 1716.

M. Alse Ware and Pemberton Proudlove, February 10, 1717/8.

B. William, son of John and Margaret Warner, September 10, 1725.

D. Mr. Nathaniel Washington, September 15, 1718.

B. Henry, son of Henry and Mary Washington, [mutilated], 1721.

B. Mildred, daughter of John and Mary Washington, August 3, 1721.

B. Anne, daughter of John and Mary Washington, November 2, 1723.

M. Townshend Washington and Elizabeth Lund, December 22, 1726.

B. Nathaniel, son of Henry and Mary Washington, January 16, 1725/6.

B. Mary, daughter of John and Mary Washington, February 28, 1725/6.

D. Mrs. Mary Washington, April 1, 1727.*

B. Susanna, daughter of Townshend and Elizabeth Washington, November 3, 1727.

B. Lawrence, son of John and Mary Washington, March 31, 1728.

B. [Completely torn away]   Washington, January 22, 1729/30.**

B. [Completely torn away]   Washington, March 10, 1729/30. ***

B. Bailey, son of Henry and Mary Washington, September 10, 1731.

B. Thomas, son of Townshend and Elizabeth Washington, March 24, 1730/1.

B. Frances, daughter of John and Mary Washington, October 20, 1731.

B. Townshend, son of Townshend and Elizabeth Washington, September 21, 1733.

B. John, son of John and Mary Washington, August 10, 1734.

D. Mary, wife of Mr. Henry Washington, January 19, 1734/5.

D. John, son of John and Mary Washington, February 13, 1735/6.

B. Townshend, son of Townshend and Elizabeth Washington, February 25, 1735/6.

B. Lund, son of Townshend and Elizabeth Washington, October 21, 1737.

---

*   This death is recorded under 1727, but may be 1727, 1728, or 1729 as no precise year is again indicated until 1730.
**   Probably Robert Washington, son of Townshend and Elizabeth Washington, who was born January 25, 1729/30 according to his Prayer Book record.
*** Probably John Washington, son of Captain Henry and Mary Washington, who is known to have been born in Saint Paul's Parish about this time, and died there at his plantation "Hylton" in 1782.

B. Elizabeth, daughter of Captain John and Mary Washington, December 21, 1737.

M. John Washington and Margaret Storke, November 23, 1738.

B. John and Lawrence, twin sons of Townshend and Elizabeth Washington, March 14, 1739/40.

B. Katherine, daughter of Captain John and Mary Washington, January 13, 1740/1.

D. Captain John Washington, February 27, 1741/2.

B. Henry, son of Townshend and Elizabeth Washington, August 29, 1742.

B. Sarah, daughter of Captain John and Mary Washington, October 28, 1742.

M. Mildred Washington and Langhorn Dade, February 14, 1742/3.

M. Henry Washington, Junior, and Elizabeth Storke, May 18, 1743.

D. Mr. Townshend Washington, December 31, 1743.

B. Lawrence, son of Henry and Elizabeth Washington, February 10, 1743/4.

D. Nathaniel, son of Captain Henry Washington, November 28, 1745.

D. Mary Washington, Junior, May 11, 1746.

D. Mary, widow of Nathaniel Washington, October 23, 1747.

D. Captain Henry Washington, October 22, 1748.

B. William, son of John and Margaret Washington, December 9, 1748.

M. Bailey Washington and Catherine Storke, January 12, 1748/9.

M. John Washington and Betty Massey, November 17, 1749.

B. Henry, son of Bailey and Catherine Washington, December 5, 1749.

M. Lawrence Washington and Elizabeth Dade, July 31, 1751.

M. Frances Washington and Charles Stuart, February 23, 1752.

B. George, son of Lawrence and Elizabeth Washington, January 4, 1758.

B. Thomas, son of Robert and Alice Washington, September 5, 1758.

M. Elizabeth Washington and Thomas Berry, November 19, 1758.

M. John Washington and Catherine Washington, December 23, 1759.

B. William Strother, son of Robert and Alice Washington, April 20, 1760.

B. Henry, son of John and Catherine Washington, October 26, 1760.

M. Elizabeth Washington and John Buckner, December 21, 1760.

B. Anne, daughter of Robert and Alice Washington, November 10, 1761.

M. Margaret Washington and Andrew Monroe, December 21, 1761.

B. Nathaniel, son of John and Catherine Washington, October [blank], 1762.

B. Townshend, son of Robert and Alice Washington, February 20, 1764.

B. Mary, daughter of John and Catherine Washington, June 17, 1764.

B. Ferdinand, son of Samuel and Anne Washington, July 16, 1767.

B. Frances Townshend, daughter of Lawrence and Elizabeth Washington, August 18, 1767.

B. Lund, son of Robert and Alice Washington, September 25, 1767.

M. Nathaniel Washington and Sarah Hooe, December 17, 1767.

M. Mary T. Washington and Robert Stith, July 29, 1773.

M. Lawrence Washington and Catherine Foote, October 5, 1774.

M. Henry Washington and Mildred Pratt, March 12, 1779.

M. Anne Washington and Thomas Hungerford, June 22, 1780.

M. Anne Washington and John Stith, December 11, 1783.

M. Anne Washington and William Thompson, August 5, 1785.

M. Thornton Washington and Frances Washington, April 2, 1786.

M. John Washington and Eleanor Massey, December 24, 1787.

M. Frances Townshend Washington and Griffin Stith, June 14, 1788.

M. Betsy Washington and Nathan Smith, April 4, 1790.

M. John Watson and Sarah Addison, February 27, 1790.

D. George Watt, August 22, 1730.

M. John Waugh and Jane Massey, April 22, 1761.

M. Gracey Waugh and Elisha Perry, January 30, 1783.

M. John Waugh and Mary Watts Ashton, November 4, 1790.

M. Elizabeth Weedon of Washington Parish and the Reverend Robert McCulloh, February 17, 1734/5.

M. John Welch and Mary Hudson, November 16, 1727.

M. Robert Welch and Elizabeth Yates, August 12, 1729.

D. John, son of Samuel Wells, August 10, 1716.

D. Samuel Wells, September 9, 1716.

M. John Wells and Frances Barnfather, June 18, 1723.

M. Samuel Wells and Susanna Brandigen, July 8, 1723.

B. Thomas, son of John and Frances Wells, September 10, 1724.

B. Anthony, son of Samuel and Susanna Wells, February 27, 1725/6.

B. John, son of John and Frances Wells, February 12, 1727/8.

D. Helenor Wells, December 15, 1729.

B. [Mutilated] of Samuel and Susanna Wells, May 2, 1730.

B. Charles, son of Samuel and Susanna Wells, May 12, 1731.

M. Charles Wells and Mary Edwards, December 10, 1733.

B. Samuel, son of Charles and Mary Wells, September 16, 1734.

B. James Penny, son of Jeremiah and Elizabeth Wetherly, December 26, 1753.

M. Elizabeth Wharton and Thomas Settle, February 26, 1778.

M. Patty Wharton and William Johnston, August 5, 1778.

M. John Whitcraft and Mary Magdelene Declore, September 25, 1716.

M. John White and Elizabeth Smith, November 12, 1730.

M. Behethlem White and Samuel Kelly, August 25, 1741.

M. Lovel White and Sarah Thomas, December 14, 1749.

M. Sarah White of King George County and George Arnold, November 9, 1758.

M. Nathan Skipweth White and Mary Burgess, April 15, 1759.

B. Roderick, son of Nathan Skipweth and Mary White, October 3, 1760.

M. Anne White and George Nash, January 20, 1769.

M. Alexander White and Priscilla Flower, April 30, 1775.

M. Mary White and William Thomas, December 13, 1785.

M. John White and Dolly Peed, January 3, 1790.

M. Bartlett White and Elizabeth Mardus, March 2, 1792.

M. Anderson White and Mary Brauner, October 14, 1794.

B. Anne, daughter of Isaac and Elizabeth Whiting, August 5, 1715.

B. Mary, daughter of Isaac and Elizabeth Whiting, April 18, 1718.

B. Samuel, son of Isaac and Elizabeth Whiting, September 14, 1723.

D. Sarah Whiting, January 28, 1723/4.

D. Isaac Whiting, December 15, 1725.

M. Mary Whiting and John Stephens, February 24, 1725/6.

B. Anne Whiting, March 25, 1737.

M. Samuel Whiting and Jane Kelly, August 29, 1744.

B. Richard, son of Samuel and Jane Whiting, January 24, 1744/5.

M. Samuel Whiting and Sarah Hall, October 5, 1750.

M. Maxfield Whiting and Lettice Johnson, February 3, 1753.

B. John, son of Mackfield [Maxfield] and Lettice Whiting, February 6, 1755.

M. Martha Whiting and Daniel Findleston, February 10, 1755.

B. Mary, daughter of John and Mary Whiting, February 10, 1756.

M. Sarah Whiting and Thomas Duncum, June 2, 1758.

B. Elizabeth, daughter of John and [blank] Whiting, September 9, 1758.

B. John, son of Samuel and Sarah Whiting, January 17, 1759.

B. George, son of Maxfield and Lettice Whiting, December 20, 1761.

M. Martha Whiting and Benjamin Derrick, January 31, 1763.

M. Mary Whiting and George Boyle, June 2, 1778.

M. Ann Whiting and John Beattie, September 10, 1779.

M. John Whiting and Nancy Gouldie, October 25, 1785.

M. Sarah Whiting and Lovell Massey, December 28, 1786.

M. John Whiting and Mildred Jones, December 26, 1788.

M. John Whiting and Mary McBean, August 10, 1791. [King George County Mar-
    riage Register gives the name of the bride as Mary Mackbaine.]

M. John Whitledge of Hamilton Parish and Elizabeth Overhall of this Parish,
    September 15, 1733.

M. Nathaniel Whitledge of Hamilton Parish and Frances Overhall of this
    Parish, October 27, 1733.

M. Lydia Whitridge of Hanover Parish and Thomas Green, March 24, 1745/6.

M. William Whitmore and Molly Carver, January 5, 1781.

D. Henry Widgeon, January 27, 1725/6.

B. Elizabeth, daughter of John and Anne Wiggin, March 9, 1758.

M. [Blank] Wiggins and [blank] Rogers, August 12, 1787.

M. Elizabeth Wiggins and Benjamin Mehorner, October 24, 1790.

B. Grace, daughter of William and Mary Wilford, May 7, 1723.

D. Grace, daughter of William and Mary Wilford, August 30, 1723.

D. William Wilford, November 13, 1726.

B. Grace, daughter of William and Mary Wilford, April 29, 1727.

D. Mary Wilford, July 24, 1738.

M. Mary Wilkerson and James Jones, April 6, 1786. [King George County
    Marriage Register states the bride is a widow.]

WILKINSON : WILKISON

M. John Wilkison and Sarah Ross, November 13, 1730.

B. William, son of John and Sarah Wilkison, October 14, 1731.

B. John, son of John and Sarah Wilkison, February 20, 1733/4.

D. Sarah Wilkison, March 3, 1733/4.

M. Samuel Wilkinson and Mary Cotes, December 9, 1734.

M. John Wilkison and Katherine Copley, August 14, 1743.

B. Barnaby, son of William and Helena Williams, March 10, 1716/7.

B. Thomas, son of Thomas and Sarah Williams deceased, February 15, 1717/8.

D. Sarah, wife of Thomas Williams, April 22, 1718.

B. Jacob Williams, May 5, 1723.

M. Thomas Williams and Helen Morphew, September 4, 1723.

D. Helena Williams, October 6, 1725.

M. Sarah Williams and Bryant Hendley, December 28, 1726.

M. Frances Williams and Paul Sweeny, December 24, 1728.

M. George Williams and Alice Fowler of Brunswick Parish, December 31, 1734.

M. Anne Williams and John Bateman, February 4, 1740/1.

B. Elizabeth, daughter of Alexander and Anne Williams, March 10, 1742/3.

M. William Williams and Mildred Duncomb, December 8, 1743.

M. Thomas Williams and Janet Johnson, November 13, 1744.

M. Thomas Williams and Anne Floyd, December 23, 1744.

B. John, son of Alexander and Anne Williams, February 1, 1745/6.

B. John, son of John and Mary Williams, January 22, 1746/7.

M. Jacob Williams and Elizabeth Miller, December 3, 1747.

B. James, son of James and Elizabeth Williams, January 11, 1774.

M. James Williams and Molly Price, April 24, 1782.

M. Walter Williamson and Mildred Dade, March 1, 1755.

B. Margaret, daughter of Walter and Mildred Williamson, October 6, 1755.*

---

* Under this entry someone has written: "Died November 18, 1837 - My
grandmother." Margaret Williamson (1755-1837) was the eldest child of
Doctor Walter Williamson and his wife nee Mildred Washington (1721—
1784) whose first husband was Langhorne Dade, Gentleman. She married
first William Robinson and secondly Colonel John Rose and left issue
by each husband. Her daughter Margaret Robinson (1780-1808) married
first in 1797 Daniel McCarty and secondly in 1802 Richard Stuart, Esq.

B. Walter, son of Walter and Mildred Williamson, November 13, 1758.

B. Mildred, daughter of Walter and Mildred Williamson, April 2, 1762.

M. John Willis and Elizabeth Plunket of Hanover Parish, January 17, 1734/5.

B. Mary Willis, a mulatto, May 2, 1747.

M. Anne Willis and James Ward, June 29, 1777.

M. Richard Wilson and Anne Smith, October 31, 1722.

B. William, son of Thomas and Ann Wilson, June 7, 1726.

B. John, son of Richard and Anne Wilson, November 11, 1726.

B. Anne, daughter of Richard and Elizabeth Wilson, January 30, 1736/7.

B. John, son of John and Anne Wilson, February 12, 1738/9.

B. Richard, son of Richard and Elizabeth Wilson, September 7, 1739.

B. Thomas, son of Richard and Elizabeth Wilson, October 21, 1744.

M. John Wilson and Jane Wood, February 12, 1750/1.

M. Benjamin Wilson and Alinda McDonald, February 27, 1757.

B. Andrew, son of Benjamin and Alinda Wilson, December 14, 1757.

M. John Wilson and Anne Lambert, October 28, 1759.

B. Mary, daughter of Benjamin and Eleanor Wilson, September 21, 1760.

B. Francis, son of William and Catherine Wilson, October 7, 1772.

M. Nelly Wilson and William Lord, April 7, 1780.

M. Catherine Wilson and Aaron Owens, March 26, 1785.

WINSON   SEE: VINCENT : VINSON   [Pages 145 and 146]

M. William Winters and Caty Hooe, November 1, 1781.

M. Martha Withers and James McDonald, November 15, 1732.

M. Lettice Woaker and John Duncan, September 27, 1735.

M. Elijah Wood and Jane Powell, June 30, 1722.

B. Mary, daughter of Elijah and Mary Wood, June 11, 1727.

D. Richard Wood, November 23, 1729.

B. Jane, daughter of Elijah and Jane Wood, January 28, 1730/1.

B. Sarah, daughter of Elijah and Jane Wood, April 17, 1733.

D. Elijah Wood, March 7, 1733/4.

D. Jane, widow of Elijah Wood, March 11, 1733/4.

M. Jane Wood and Matthew Dyal, January 23, 1738/9.

M. Mary Wood and Malcolm McIntosh, November 24, 1743.

M. Jane Wood and John Wilson, February 12, 1750/1.

M. Sarah Worldey and John Shotwell, June 26, 1725.

B. William, son of William and Sarah Worley, March 30, 1761.

B. John, son of William and Mary Worrel, September 2, 1737.

B. William, son of William and Mary Worrel, August 13, 1740.

B. Mary, daughter of William and Mary Worrel, April 19, 1743.

B. Philip, son of William and Mary Worrel, June 16, 1746.

M. William Worton and Margaret Hamilton, February 26, 1724/5.

D. Margaret Worton, January 24, 1725/6.

M. Jacob Wray and Mary Ashton, May 13, 1761.

M. Helen Wray and Charles Stuart, October 31, 1783.

M. Mary Wray and John Alexander Stuart, November 17, 1785.

D. Mottrom Wright, November 26, 1729.

M. Francis Wright and Anne Massey, December 7, 1737.

M. John Lewright [? John Lee Wright?] and Mary Kitchen, August 8, 1751.
    [See also page 84.]

Y

YARENTHARP   SEE: ALLENTHROPE : ALLENTRAP : ALINTRAP   [Page 3]

M. Ann Yarentharp and John Smith, March 7, 1748/9.

M. Elizabeth Yates and Robert Welch, August 12, 1729.

M. James Yates of Sittenbourne Parish and Mary Green of Washington Parish,
    November 19, 1745.

M. Robert Yates and Elizabeth Dade, February 17, 1750/1.

B. Robert, son of Robert and Elizabeth Yates, July 22, 1752.

B. Henry, son of Robert and Elizabeth Yates, January 10, 1754.

B. Charles, son of Robert and Elizabeth Yates, August 5, 1756.

B. Henry Francis Dade, son of Robert and Elizabeth Yates, August 20, 1765.

M. Robert Yates and Jane Dade, April 11, 1777.

M. William Young and Elizabeth Griggs, August 29, 1746.

B. William, son of William Young, October 19, 1753.

B. Eleanor, daughter of William and Elizabeth Young, March 2, 1757.

B. David, son of William and Elizabeth Young, February 15, 1759.

Z

ZACHARY [?]   See: SACHARY   [Page 118]

F I N I S